The Bavarian Army 1806-1813

Peter Bunde
Markus Gärtner
Markus Stein

Translated by Richard L. Sanders

Dedicated to our friend and mentor Edmund Wagner (1938-2011)

Lieutenant of the Army Transport System (*Armeefuhrwesen*), 1815
Watercolor by Edmund Wagner after Louis Braun,
From the collection of Edmund Wagner

We thank Patrice Courcelle for the production of both plates, Erik Bauer for the maps, Pierre-Yves Chauvin and Hans-Karl Weiß for the critical review of the manuscript and Peter Harrington, Curator of the Ann S. K. Brown Library in Providence, Rhode Island, for the permission to reproduce numerous plates.

Authors: Markus Gärtner & Markus Stein
Uniform plates: Peter Bunde
Maps: Bernhard Glänzer
Translation: Richard L. Sanders

Editor & Layout: Stefan Müller

Publisher: Zeughaus Verlag GmbH
Knesebeckstr. 88, 10623 Berlin

Telephone: 0049 (0)30/315 700 30
Fax: 0049 (0)30/315 700 77
Email: info@zeughausverlag.de
Website: www.zeughausverlag.de

Bibliographic Information from the Deutschen Bibliothek: The Deutsche Bibliothek lists this publication in the German National Bibliography; detailed bibliographic Information is available at http://dnb.ddb.de.Bibliografische Informationen der Deutschen Bibliothek.
All rights reserved. No part of this publication my be reproduced, stored in or introduced into a retrieval system, or transmitted, in any form, or by any means (electronic, mechanical, photocopying, recording or otherwise) without the prior written permission of the publisher. Any person who does any unauthorized act in relation to this publication may be liable to criminal prosecution and civil claims for damages.

Printed in European Union

© 2018 Zeughaus Verlag GmbH

ISBN: 978-3-938447-99-4

Contents

INTRODUCTION 8

ORGANIZATION
    Composition of the Army 9
    General Officers and Military Administration 10
    Infantry 12
    Cavalry 18
    Technical Troops 24
    Other Branches 28

UNIFORMS
    Introduction 30
    Rank Insignia 30
    General Officers and Staff 30
    Field Jaeger Corps – 1805 to 1808 34
    Cadet Corps 34
    Hartschiere Court Guard-Body Guard 35

    Infantry
    Infantry of the Line 35
    Light Infantry Battalions 43
    Tyrolean Jaeger Battalion 48
    Garrison Troops 48

    Cavalry
    Dragoons, until 1811 48
    Chevaulegers 50
    Regiments' Horse Colors 58
    The National Chevauleger Regiment –
    starting 1813 the 7th Regiment Prinz Karl 58

Technical Troops (Royal Artillery Corps)
    Foot Artillery 60
    Light Artillery/Batteries 62
    Army Transport System 62
    Engineers 64
    Painting of Artillery Pieces 64
    Military Administration 64
    Nationalgarde 2. Klasse - Mobile Legions 68
    Military Police 68
    Field Postal Service 72
    Weapons 72
    Standards and Company Guidons 72
    Differences for the Regiments 76

REGULATIONS AND ORDERS
    Infantry 77
    Cavalry 80
    Other Branches 80

DOMESTIC SITUATION
    Recruiting and Service Obligations 81
    Awards and Military Justice 82

THE CAMPAIGNS
    The 1806-07 Campaign 86
    The 1809 Campaign 90
    Suppressing the 1809 Tyrolean Insurrection 96
    The 1812 Campaign 97
    The 1813 Campaign 102

SOURCES AND LITERATURE 107

King Maximilian-Joseph I., 1756 - 1825
Bayerisches Armeemuseum
Ingolstadt, photo: M. Gärtner

INTRODUCTION

In 1799, Maximilian Joseph took over from his predecessor, Electoral Prince (*Kurfürst*) Carl-Theodor, an army that was poorly regarded by everyone, and that shortly before Maximilian Joseph's accession totaled barely 15,000 men.[1] Also under the influence of the dominant French "new" army structures, Maximilian Joseph abandoned the absolutist traits of the Bavarian Army and pushed for its professionalization.[2] The Kingdom of Bavaria, as the largest state in the Confederation of the Rhine (*Rheinbund*)[3], provided the largest contingent with 30,000 soldiers, but in contrast to the other Confederation states, it was spared any mission in the civil war in Spain. But based on the size of its contingent, in the 1809 and 1812 campaigns Bavaria could deploy some larger divisions or army corps under partially joint leadership by French comanders-in-chief and Bavarian Generals.

---

1 For an exact listing of the strength of the army, see Friedrich Münich, page 188.

2 Among them were abolishing buying of officers' positions and founding of a military academy.

3 See the „Statistik der Rheinbundstaaten", published in Napoleon Online (http://www.napoleon-online.de/armee_rheinbundstaaten.html).

Carl, Prince of Wrede (Fürst von Wrede)
General's dress uniform, 1813
Plate from the series – Die bayerische Armee 1813-1826 by J. Volz

ORGANIZATION

Composition of the Army

The Bavarian units, in harmony with the French Army's successfully adapted army organization, were also divided into divisions and brigades. For the 1805 Campaign, the brigades were each to be made up of two Line infantry regiments, one light infantry battalion and one cavalry regiment.[4] Starting in 1806, the brigades were assigned a battery.

After the return from the 1806-07 Campaign, the units were consolidated into general commands that were named after their locations.

This structure was adjusted for the kingdom's new districts by the Army Orders of 24 September 1808 and the General Commands (*Generalkommandos*) were named after their main locations. The General Command in Bavaria became "*Generalkommando München*", that in Schwabia became Augsburg, that in Franconia became "Nürnberg" (Nuremberg) and the one in Tirol became Innsbruck.

For the exact composition of the forces in the 1806-07, 1809 and 1812-13 campaigns, refer to the chapter on the History of the Wars.

---

4   *Each Line Regiment of 2 battalions with a grenadier and 3 fusilier companies each; the light infantry battalions with 4 companies and the cavalry regiment with 4 squadrons (Münich, page 207).*

General Officers and Military Administration

In 1806, the Bavarian Army could count 22 active Lieutenant Generals and 39 active Major Generals, whose numbers were reduced by 1811 to 6 Generals, 16 Lieutenant Generals and 21 Major Generals. The newly introduced rank of General differed according to the branch of the Army.[5]

Johann Nepomuk von Triva
(20 Sept. 1755 – 8 Apr.1827)
Bavarian General and Minister of War

The Secret War Office (*Geheime Kriegsbüro*) created in 1804 under then Major General von Triva was to address the "preparation of the service, personnel and command issues of the Army and its direct presentation for the highest level decision."[6] Thus the Bavarian Army got its first General Staff structure for support to the Commander-in-Chief. The Secret War Office was disbanded through the order of 27 September 1808 and expanded to the newly formed Ministry of War, and von Triva was designated its leader in the rank of Lieutenant General. The Army Uniform[7], the Military Horse Breeding Farm (*Fohlenhof*) Schwaiganger, the Administration for Provisions, Fodder, Barracks and Dispensaries, and the General Hospital Inspection were subordinated to the Ministry of War.

For field duty, the General Staff created several Quartermaster Lieutenant Generals and several attached officers from the Quartermaster General's (*Lieutenant General von Triva's*) office.[8]

Imitating the *Guides and Gendarmes* in the French Revolutionary Army's headquarters, a *"Hunters Corps"* (*Jaegerkorps*) was created in 1805. This corps of 120 mounted and 400 foot jaegers was to be recruited primarily from foresters and hunters. They were to be settled near the headquarters and conduct scouting in the countryside, transmit orders, and perform police duties. The *Jaegerkorps* was first employed in the 1806-07 Campaign, however disbanded in 1808.

The medical service was notably enhanced by Maximilian Joseph[9] and professionalized in terms of personal and equipment. The General Hospital Inspection, created in March 1804, had the mission to regularly check the Bavarian military dispensaries and clinics, to test the doctors and surgeons employed there and to issue pharmaceutical guidelines. Dispensaries were led by directly assigned doctors and those detailed from the regiments, supported by several nurses and additional assistants and administrative personnel.[10] Starting in 1804, regimental doctors and regimental surgeons had to have completed secondary schooling (*Gynnasialabschluss*), as well as knowledge of surgery and medicine.

With the founding of the Veterinary School (*Tierarzneischule*) by Rumford in 1799, the veterinary system was already on a comparably high level before Maximilian Joseph's becoming the king. The Regulation of 19 January 1802 specified that no senior blacksmith (*Oberschmied*) could serve in the regiments without having attended the school and acquired adequate practical experience. In 1808, the Veterinary System was subordinated to the General Hospital Inspection.

The Military Chaplaincy in the Bavarian kingdom was no longer, as earlier apportioned to the regiments, but to the brigades.[11]

Very soon after becoming the Electoral Prince, Maximilian Joseph, as the Commander-in-Chief built a military administration that was to focus and execute all military activities. In 1801, the Military Justice Council (*Kriegs-Justiz-Rat*) and War Economy Council (*Kriegs-Ökonomie-Rat*)[12] were formed, additionally the 7th Deputation of the State Directorate (*Landes-Direktion*) created in

---

5   Infantry General, Cavalry General, Artillery General.

6   Regulation of 18 March 1804 (quoted in Münich, page 195).

7   The first preparations for a central depot for uniforms were laid in 1805 with consolidating the tailors of all the regiments and battalions located in Tirol and Salzburg and posting them in Munich. In 1808, a saddlery was added to the Uniform Depot. The so-called Army Uniform Depot Commission attended to all centralized supplying of uniforms and equipment and the daily wages of the workers entrusted with their production. It was also responsible for the oversight of production of uniforms according to patterns - in accordance with economical rules, i.e., the most exact adherence to the given use of material.

8   For 1807, Münich counts : 1 Quartermaster General, 3 Quartermasters Lieutenant General, 1 colonel, 2 majors, 3 captains, 2 senior lieutenants and 1 junior lieutenant.

9   This was expressed by, among other things, the Military Medical Medal (*Militär-Sanitäts-Ehrenzeichen*), created on 8 November 1812.

10   The Instructions from 1799 to 1801 established the staffing numbers for personnel besides doctors as 1 administrator and 2 administrative assistants, 4 nurses for the care and as aides 1 housekeeper, 1 female cook and severalmaids. So-called Regimental Dispensaries (*Regimentslazarette*) were to be under the oversight of retired NCOs.

11   In the 1809 campaign, the 1st Division was assigned 2 Catholic, the 2nd Division had 2 Catholic and 1 Protestant and the 3rd Division had 2 Catholic and 1 Protestant Field Chaplains.

12   In the 1811 Army Service List (*Rangliste*) the War Economy Council was authorized 1 Director, 6 Councilors (*Räte*), 4 Secretaries, 3 Registrars and 2 Expediters.

Evolution of the Bavarian infantry uniform with the 9th Infantry Regiment as an example
From left to right 1778-1785, then 1789-1799, then 1806, then 1812-1814 (from Käuffer 1895)

1799 dealt with numerous matters of military administration.[13] The Military Justice Council was converted a General Auditing Office in 1804 that dealt with military jurisdiction issues.[14] Furthermore, there was a Military Main Accounting Office (*Kriegs-Haupt-Buchhalterei*) for the entire pay system as well as a Main Military Pay office (*Militär-Haupt-Kasse*).

The *"Instruction on the Administration and Rear Area Services of the Grand Armee"* issued by Napoleon in preparation for the 1812 campaign authorized the creation of field postal service in divisions. The Bavarian order of 28 March 1812 established the creation of a Field Post Office with two Field Postal Officials, two letter carriers and four field messengers.[15]

In 1807, in order to reduce the dependence on foreign horse sellers, the generals decided to establish their own Bavarian horse breeding farm in addition to the one in Poland. This was set up in the Schwaiganger royal property and stocked with foals.[16] However, due to an attack by Tyrolean rebels in 1809 the efforts were hindered so that horses had to be obtained from non-Bavarian regions.[17]

---

13 The procurement of uniforms, provisioning of troops, or the pay system, among other things.

14 According to the Army Service List 1811 with 1 Chief, 1 Vice-Chief, 2 General Auditors, 3 Senior Auditors, 1 Presidential Secretary and 2 Secretaries.

15 For the Field Postal Service's activities in the 1812 campaign, see Fabrice, pages 310-311.

16 Selected Moldauer studs from the 1st (later 3rd) Chevaulegers Regiment were covered for this purpose and their foals were delivered to the new military horse breeding farm.

17 This circumstance also underscores the number of 1.152 horses that went to the Bavarian Army from the farm between 1818 and 1823 (peacetime!), while in the same period another 925 remounts had to be purchased (see Münich, page 234).

General Staff Officer, 1812

C.F. Weiland, *Die französische Armee und ihre Alliierten*.

Lipperheide Series, Kostümbibliothek Berlin, photo: M. Stein

Infantry

The Royal Bodyguards (*königliche Leibgarde*), was made up of the *"Hartschiere"* created in 1669, whose mounted section had been disbanded, as well as the *"Trabanten"*. The latter were disbanded in 1807, into which some of the Hartschiere had been encorporated.

The Bavarian infantry was divided in Line Infantry Regiments and Light Infantry Battalions, the latter having been created in 1801 from the old Feldjäger Regiments.

The *"Rangliste"* for the Line Infantry Regiments and Light Infantry Battalions were structured as follows per the Army Order of 10 March 1804:	
Line Infantry Regiments	**Light Infantry Battalions**
No. 1 Leibregiment	No. 1 Metzen
No. 2 Kurprinz (after 1/1/1806 Kronprinz)	No. 2 Vincenti
No. 3 Herzog Carl	No. 3 Preysing
No. 4 Weichs	No. 4 Stengel
No. 5 Preysing	No. 5 de Lamotte
No. 6 Herzog Wilhelm	No. 6 Weinbach
No. 7 Morawitzky	
No. 8 Herzog Pius	
No. 9 Ysenburg	
No. 10 Junker	
No. 11 Kinkel	
No. 12 Löwenstein	

Through the reorganization of the Bavarian Army into brigades in September 1805, excess soldiers were reallocated to the newly formed 13th Infantry Regiment.[18]

In reaction to the *"desertion"*[19] of numerous soldiers of the 12th Line Infantry Regiment Loewenstein the number 12 was no longer listed in the Army Service List starting 31 May 1806 and the remaining soldiers formed the 14th Line Infantry.

By the transfer of the 11th Line Infantry Regiment Kinkel to the Grand Duchy of of Berg in December 1806, the 11th Regiment was raised again in July 1807.[20]

---

18 Predominantly from Regiments No. 9 and No. 12.

19 After the founding of the Grand Duchy of Wuerzburg, the soldiers who came from Wuerzburg and had been in serving in Bavaria since 1803 in the 12th Regiment wanted to return home, but were prevented from doing so and taken prisoner by their French allie (Münich, pages 242-243).

20 The 1st Battalion was formed from four companies of the 1st, 5th, 6th and 8th Line Infantry Regiments; the 2nd Battalion from four companies of the 2nd, 4th, 7th and 10th Line Infantry Regiments.

On 7 May 1807, a Tyrolean Jaeger Battalion was created based on volunteers and it consisted of four companies and a total of 888 men. An order from 24 March 1808 order enlarged the Jaeger formation to five companies and renamed it as the 7th Light Infantry Battalion Guenter.

After April 1811, Line Infantry Regiment No. 1 took over the *"König"* (King) designation while Regiment No. 11 Kinkel and the 7th Light Infantry Battalion (named Treuberg then) were disbanded. Regiment No. 13 took over the number 11 and received Lieutenant General Baron Kinkel as the commander and then Regiment No. 14 received the number 13.

In the same way, in April 1811, the Garrison regiments were re-designated as Garrison Companies and named after their locations: Donauwoerth, Nymphenburg, Oberhaus, Rosenberg, Rothenburg and Wuerzburg.

After 12 May 1803, the Line Infantry Regiments were reorganized into two battalions five companies each, one of which was a grenadier company. After 31 March 1804, the strengths were fixed at 2,692 men for a Line Infantry Regiment, and with the half strength of 1352 men for a light infantry battalion. The following table[21] lists the distribution of ranks within both infantry formations based on authorized strengths:

		Line Infantry	Light Battalion
Staff	Proprietor	1	-
	Colonel-Commandant (w/ 3 horses each)	1	-
	Lieutenant Colonel (w/ 2 horses each)	1	1
	Major (w/ 2 horses each)	2	1
	Adjutant (w/ 1 horse each)	2	1
	Junker	2	1
Lower Staff	Regimental (Battalion) Quartermaster	1	1
	Auditor	1	1
	Regimental Surgeon	1	-
	Junior Surgeon	2	1
	Surgeon's Assistant	2	1
	Regimental (Battalion) Drummer	1	1
	Oboist (*Hautboist*)	10	10
	Provost with Assistant	2	2
	Rifle Maker	1	1
2 Battalions	Captain (*Hauptmann*)	5	3
	Captain (*Capitän*)	5	3
	Senior Lieutenant	10	5
	Junior Lieutenant	20	10
	Master Sergeant (*Feldwebel*)	10	5
	Quartermaster sergeant (*Furier*)	10	5
	Sergeant	20	10
	Corporal	60	30
	Piper	2	-
	Drummer	20	10
	Senior Private (*Gefreiter*)	120	60
	Privat (*Gemeiner*)	2.380	1.190

From the authorized strength one can infer that a company included 1 Captain or *"Hauptmann"*, 1 Senior Lieutenant, 2 Junior Lieutenants, 1 *"Feldwebel,"* 1 *"Furier"*, 2 Sergeants, 6 Corporals, 2 drummers, 12 senior privates (*"Gefreite"*) and 238 privates (*"Gemeine"*). According to regulations, a Line Infantry Regiment should go to the field with 2,000 men and a Light Infantry Battalion with 1,000 men, the remainder would remain at the replacement depot. After April 1804, two reserve companies were formed from a Line Infantry Regiment's remaining

Helmet for Officers of the Light Jaeger, 1815

Bayerisches Armeemuseum Ingolstadt,
photo: M. Gaertner

---

21 The table shows the service ranks as they were written at that time.

soldiers, and one reserve company from a Light Infantry Battalion.[22]

Each Regiment could bring four, and the Light Infantry Battalion two cadets into their ranks of their non-commissioned officers (NCOs) or privates.

Starting 31 March 1804, one sapper ("*Zimmermann*") and 20 sharpshooters ("*Schützen*"), including 6 senior sharpshooters ("*Schützen-Gefreite*"), were designated in each company. Henceforth, out of the regiment's or battalion's 10 oboists, 2 were designated buglers to serve as signalers for the sharpshooters.

Starting on 31 March 1804, each infantry regiment was to carry only one *"Leibfahne"* and one *"Ordinärfahne"* (ordinary flag).

The 1805 reorganization of the Bavarian Army into six brigades led to a reduction of the company strength to 155 soldiers and at the same time a reduction in the number of companies per battalion. Line infantry regiments now included one grenadier and three fusilier companies; light infantry battalions had four companies. The resulting excess soldiers were distributed to the newly created 13th Line Infantry. Regiment and the depot companies.

The combat strength per company was increased to 185 soldiers by the Army Order of 15 September 1806. Each company was divided into four platoons (*Züge*) each with 20 troops and five sharpshooters.[23]

Per the directive of 10 October 1806, the regiments were authorized to take along at least two women per company to the field.

After 12 August 1808, each line infantry regiment was to consist of two grenadier and six fusilier companies; the light infantry battalions of four companies. The combat strength of a company was now set at 180 men.

The 9 March 1809 Army Order, which increased the sharpshooters to one-fifth of the company strength (i.e., 36 sharpshooters) by ordering the filling in with companies' qualified men, took the need for skirmishers into account. Therefore, each battalion was assigned an additional junior lieutenant as the second officer, and a bugler and each company got two vice corporals (*Vizekorporäle*) for the sharpshooters.

Based on the numerous forces available from the war of 1809, on 8 May 1809, King Maximilian Joseph ordered the creation of six reserve battalions from the reserve companies remaining in the country to use for national defense. Each of this battalions was to consist of four companies, these included 3 officers, 1 *Feldwebel*, 1 quartermaster sergeant (*Furier*), 2 sergeants, 6 corporals, 2 drummers, 10 senior privates and 110 privates. The reserve battalion staff had 1 battalion commander, 1 adjutant, 1 quartermaster, 1 battalion surgeon, 1 general practitioner, 1 battalion drum major and 2 provosts (*Profoße*) with assistants.[24]

On 25 June 1809, during the ceasefire between the battles of Aspern-Essling and Wagram, the king ordered the reserve battalions to be increased to 12. At the same time, the old regimental depots were disbanded and the soldiers there were assigned to the respective reserve battalions. From this timepoint, each line infantry regiment was to have a reserve battalion of four fusilier companies – at the same strength as the companies of the field battalions. By order, the reserve battalions were assigned the status of National Guard 1st Class (*Nationalgarde 1. Klasse*).

On 1 October 1810, the practice of naming companies after their commanders was abolished and a numbering system was introduced in its stead. Each battalion was too have one company designated as its reserve.

The Army Orders of 29 April 1811 brought a completely new organization of the regiments' and battalions' structures. The resulting 12 line infantry regiments were now to include two field battalions with six companies each (1 grenadier, 1 sharpshooter (*Schützen*) and 4 fusilier companies) and one reserve battalion of four companies. Each company had 150 men, the regiment thus reached an authorized strength of 2,436 men. The resulting six light infantry battalions had 1 carabinier, 1 *Schützen*, 4 fusilier and 2 reserve fusilier companies, each with 150 men. The battalion totaled 1,224 men. The following table lists the distribution of the ranks in the staff and each company of the line infantry regiments and light infantry battalions.

---

[22] These Reserve Companies served not only as sources of replacements for their parent units in the field, and trainers for recruits, but also carried out police duties at home.

[23] See also the changes of the infantry from the two-rank to three-rank formation and the positioning of the sharpshooters in the section regulations on pages 73 to 75.

[24] All reserve battalions' soldiers were to wear the "old" uniforms, which based on the assignment of the line infantry regiments existing in the field resulted with: the 1st Reserve Battalion wore the uniform of the Regiment No. 1; the 2nd Battalion had that of Regiment No. 4; the 3rd Battalion wore that of Regiment No. 3; the 4th Battalion got that of Regiment No. 5; the 5th battalion received that of Regiment No. 13; and the 6th Battalion wore that of Regiment No. 9.

		Line infantry	Light Battalion
Staff	Commanding Colonel	1	-
	Lieutenant Colonel	1	1
	Major	2	1
	Adjutant	3	1
	Junker	3	1
	Staff Regimental (Battalion) Quartermaster	1	1
	Regimental (Battalion) Auditor	1	1
	Regimental (Battalion) Surgeon	3	2
	Surgeon's Assistant	3	2
	1st Music Master and Oboists[25]	13	11
	Regimental Drummer	1	-
	Battalion Drummer	1	1
	Provost	1	1
	Rifle Maker	1	1
All companies (16 in the Line Infantry Regiment, 8 in the Light Infantry Battalion)	Captain 1st Class	6	3
	Captain 2nd Class	10	5
	Senior Lieutenant	16	8
	Junior Lieutenant	16	8
	Master Sergeant (*Feldwebel*)	16	8
	Quartermaster sergeant (*Furier*)	16	8
	Sergeant	32	16
	Corporal	64	32
	Bugler (*Hornist*)	4	2
	Drummer	28	14
	Senior Private (*Gefreiter*)	144	72
	Private (*Gemeiner*)	2.048	1.024

Among the Senior Privates (*Gefreiten*) were 16 sappers (*Zimmerleute*)[25] in the line infantry regiment and 8 in the light infantry battalion.

From these figures, one can infer the composition of a company as:
- 1 Captain (*Capitän*),
- 1 Senior Lieutenant (*Oberlieutenant*),
- 1 Junior Lieutenant, (*Unterlieutenant*)
- 1 Master Sergeant (*Feldwebel*),
- 1 Quartermaster Sergeant (*Furier*),
- 2 Sergeants (*Sergeanten*),
- 4 Corporals (*Korporäle*),
- 2 Buglers (*Hornisten*) for the *Schützen* or 2 drummers for the other companies,
- 9 Senior Privates (*Gefreite*),
- 128 Privates (*Gemeine*)

Helmet – Caterpillar Helmet (*Raupenhelm*), Model for Troops
Bayerisches Armeemuseum Ingolstadt,
photo: M. Gaertner

---

25 "*Zimmerleute*" is the plural for "*Zimmermann*," which literally is translated as "carpenter," but in this context would be a sapper.

The Regiment Koenig (No.1) in the Battle of Polozk, 17-18 August 1812
Extract from the painting by Wilhelm von Kobell, Residenzmuseum Munich

The 1st field battalion was commanded by the colonel, the 2nd field battalion by the major and the reserve battalion by the lieutenant colonel. The second major was located near the regimental commander to rapidly replace any missing staff officer if needed.

According to the Orders of April 1811, each fusilier company was to detail an NCO and a private as a color guard.[26] Each grenadier or carabinier company detailed an NCO to the sappers.

On 6 March 1813, after the destruction of the Bavarian field forces in Russia, the king ordered the realignment of all infantry units. Those units still in one of the mobile corps were to form the first battalion of their regiment; the second battalion was created directly from the reserve battalion of its regiment. Each battalion was to consist of six companies, including one grenadier and one sharpshooter (*Schützen*) company, each with a strength of 121 men. The light infantry battalions that were in the field were to form three companies also including a combined sharpshooter-carabinier company (*Schützen-Karabinier-Kompanie*), were formed from the reserves of the light infantry battalions.

In the course of a further enhancement to the new Bavarian forces, the Order of 31 May 1813 called for the creation of as many as possible "mobile companies" each with 100 to 150 men from all the reserve battalions of the line infantry regiments and reserve divisions of the light infantry battalions.

For the period up to 1806 a line infantry regiment was authorized a wagon park of:

- 1 four-horse wagon for the regimental payroll and filing cabinet
- 1 two-horse wagon for service uniforms
- 2 two-horse open-frame wagons (*Leiterwagen*) for the surgeons and to transport medicine and up to wounded
- 6 two-horse open-frame wagons for officers' baggage
- 4 two-horse open-frame wagons for cauldrons and pots
- 2 four-horse open-frame wagons for food provisions
- 4 four-horse ammunition wagons

Per the Order of 10 October 1806, each infantry battalion was allocated two ammunition wagons, one wagon to carry the officers' baggage, an ambulance wagon and a wagon to transport shoes. Since as a rule this occurred without horses to pull them, the units had to requisition additional wagons and horse teams.

---

26 According to F. Münich, the NCO had to be able to "primarily march".

Infantry Coat, 1813-1814
Bayerisches Armeemuseum Ingolstadt, photo: M. Gaertner

Cavalry

At the time of the creation of the kingdom in the beginning of January 1806, the Bavarian Army consisted of six cavalry regiments, i.e., two dragoon as heavy cavalry and four Chevauleger as light horse regiments. They were numbered and designated as follows:
Dragoon Regiment No. 1 Minucci
Dragoon Regiment No. 2 Taxis
Chevauleger Regiment No. 1 Kronprinz
Chevauleger Regiment No. 2 Koenig
Chevauleger Regiment No. 3 Leiningen
Chevauleger Regiment No. 4 Bubenhofen

Per the Army Order of 29 April 1811, the dragoons were converted to Chevauleger regiments with the following numeric designations:
1st Chevauleger Regiment Minucci
2nd Chevauleger Regiment Taxis
3rd Chevauleger Regiment Kronprinz
4th Chevauleger Regiment Koenig
5th Chevauleger Regiment Leiningen
6th Chevauleger Regiment Bubenhofen

The Instruction (*Vorschrift*) of 16 April 1803 directed that each cavalry regiment was to consist of six squadrons (*Eskadronen*) and the divisions (*Divisionen*) of the squadrons were based on the commander's rank, i.e., the first squadron was designated the *"Leib-Eskadron"* ("Body's Squadron"), the second squadron was the *"Oberst-Eskadron"* (Colonel's Squadron), the third was the *"Oberstlieutenant-Eskadron"* (Lieutenant Colonel's Squadron), the fourth was the *"Erste Majors-Eskadron"* (1st Major's Squadron), the fifth was the *"Zweite Majors-Eskadron"* (2nd Major's Squadron), and the sixth was the *"Rittmeister [l.n.]-Eskadron"* (Cavalry Captain [last name]-Squadron).

If there was only one major in the regiment, then the 5th and 6th squadrons were commanded by cavalry captains (*Rittmeistern*).

Starting 5 May 1803, only the dragoons continued to carry two standards; the Chevauleger regiments gave up their standards.[27] To replace the two *"Standartenjunker"* NCOs, the Chevaulegers got 2 *Junker* assigned.[28] Starting in March 1804, the number of standards for the dragoons was reduced to one.

Beginning in May 1803, each cavalry regiment had the following rank structure:

		Dragoons	Chevaulegers
Staff	Proprietor (*Inhaber*)	1	1
	Colonel (*Oberst*)	1	1
	Lieutenant Colonel	1	1
	Major	1	1
	Regimental Quartermaster	1	1
	Auditor	1	1
	Adjutant	1	1
	Color Ensign	3	-
	Ensign (*Estandartjunker*)	-	2
	Regimental Surgeon	1	1
	Deputy Surgeon	2	2
	Surgeon´s Assistant	2	2
	Senior Blacksmith	1	1
	Staff Trumpeter	1	1
	Provost and Assistant	2	2
Each Squadron	Captain (*Rittmeister*)	1	1
	Senior Lieutenant	1	1
	Junior Lieutenant	2	2
	Master Sergeant	1	1
	Quartermaster NCO	1	1
	Sergeant	1	1
	Corporal	6	6
	Trumpeter	2	2
	Blacksmith	1	1
	Saddler	1	1
	Troope	132	132

If there was a second major in the regiment, he was counted under the number for captains (*Rittmeister*).

The Army order of 31 March 1804 authorized colonels 6 horses, lieutenant colonels and majors 4 horses, the captains (*Rittmeistern*) 3 horses and lieutenants 2 horses. The regiment was additionally allocated a total of 400 horses. In addition, each regiment was authorized 2 cadets.

The strength of a squadron was increased by the orders of 31 March 1804 to 180 privates (*Gemeine*), of whom only 150 were to go to the field. The remaining soldiers from the squadrons were consolidated in the reserve squadrons.[29]

According to the Army Order of 15 April 1806, a cavalry regiment's authorized horses were to be increased to 660, i.e., 110 per squadron.

27　Chevauleger recruits were sworn in "on the sword" rather than "on the standard." The dragoons did not carry their standards in the field.

28　The order described the Junker as "Individuals who are to be employed as non-commissioned officers, but who are also to be trained to be efficient officers." (Quoted from F. Münich, page 263.)

29　Similar to the infantry's reserve companies and battalions, the cavalry's reserve squadrons were not only supposed to accept able-bodied cadets and train new recruits, but also be able to provide security and maintain order inside Bavaria.

Officer's Helmet, Regiment Taxis No. 2
Bayerisches Armeemuseum Ingolstadt, Photo: Bayerisches Armeemuseum Ingolstadt

National Chevauleger Regiment, No. 7

From the series "Die bayerische Armee 1813-1826", by J. Volz

Lieutenant General Wrede's degree on 22 April 1806 introduced so-called "mobile divisions" that were made up as follows: 1st (*Oberst-*) division, consisting of the *Leib* squadron and the *Oberst* squadron, and the 3rd (Major's) Division, composed of the 2nd major's squadron and the *Rittmeister* squadron. The so-called "immobile division" retained the 2nd (*Oberstlieutenant-*) division from the *Oberstlieutenant* squadron and the 1st Major's squadron. Each mobile squadron included 1 *Rittmeister*, 1 senior lieutenant, 2 junior lieutenants, 2 master sergeants (*Wachtmeister*), 1 Furier, 6 corporals, 2 vice-corporals (*Vizekorporäle*), 2 trumpeters, 1 blacksmith (*Schmied*), 1 saddler and 95 privates. Thus both mobile divisions of a regiment reached an authorized strength of 380 privates and 449 service horses.

The cavalry was also limited by the order of 10 October 1806 to being able to only take "at most" two women per squadron to the field.

After the conversion of the dragoon regiments to Chevaulegers on 29 April 1811, each regiment was to have a strength of 1,068 men and 875 horses.

On 6 March 1813, after the destruction of the Bavarian cavalry in the 1812 Russia campaign, Maximilian Joseph ordered the reestablishment of the six old regiments. Initially the 1st division was to be raised again from the 1st and 2nd squadrons each with 109 Chevaulegers and 125 horses per squadron. Once the 1st division reached its authorized strength, the 2nd and 3rd divisions were to be created successively. After that, all further recruits and deliveries of horses were assigned to reserve squadrons.

At the beginning of the 19th century, the Bavarian Army's cavalry regiments were almost exclusively mounted on horses from Germany. After the 1806-07 campaign King Maximilian Joseph had numerous horses purchased in Prussian and Poland so that about one third of the regiments' horses were from Poland. Because the Schwaiganger horse breeding farm (see section on Military Administration) could barely meet the need for horses, starting in 1813 Moldavian horses were exclusively purchased.[30]

---

30 *These were driven in herds to Bavaria and then distributed to the regiments in Munich. For each horse that reached the Bavarian border, a fee of 28 Dutch ducats was charged (F. Münich, page 271).*

Scale Epaulettes for Cavalry and Artillery
Stadtmuseum Abensberg
photo: M. Gaertner

Campaign Frock Coat of Colonel Karl Freiherr Ditfurth, 11th Infantry Regiment, 1809
Bayerisches Armeemuseum Ingolstadt
photo: Bayerisches Armeemuseum Ingolstadt

Feldjaeger; Chevauleger Regiment Taxis and 1st Dragoon Regiment up to 1811

Augsburger Bilderserie, Universität- und Landesbibliothek Darmstadt

Officers of the 1st Chevauleger and 2nd Dragoon Regiments up to 1811
Augsburger Bilderserie, Universität- und Landesbibliothek Darmstadt

Technical Troops (*Technische Truppen*)

During Maximilian Joseph's reign the artillery was extensively reorganized, primarily based on Lieutenant General Manson's ideas.[31] The Technical Executive Committee (*technische Leitungsgremium*) sat in the Arsenal Main Directorate (*Zeughaus-Hauptdirektion*)[32] and was directly under Manson's command.

According to the regulations from March 1804, the artillery was organized as an artillery regiment. It consisted of three battalions with 11 (foot) Artillery and one Worker (*Ouvrier*) company, completed with one company of horse artillery.

The Regiment had the following authorized strength:

Staff	Regimental Proprietor (6 horses)	1
	Colonel-Commandant (2 horses)	1
	Lieutenant Colonel (2 horses)	1
	Major (2 horses each)	3
	Adjutant General (1 horse)	1
	Adjutant (1 horse each)	2
Lower staff	Regimental Quartermaster	1
	Auditor	1
	Regimental Surgeon	1
	Deputy Surgeon	3
	Surgeon´s Assitant	3
	Munitions Superindant (*Munitionär*)	1
	Regimental Drummer	1
	Provost and Assistant	2
11 (Foot) Artillery Companies (according to Regulations of 23 March 1804)	Senior Captain (*Hauptmann*)	5
	Junior Captain (*Capitän*)	6
	Senior Lieutenant	11
	Junior Lieutenant	22
	Master Sergeant (*Oberfeuerwerker*)	11
	Quartermaster Sergeant (*Furier*)	11
	Bombardier-Corporal	22
	Kanonier-Corporal	88
	Drummer	22
	Bombardier 1st Class	132
	Bombardier 2nd Class	88
	Artilleryman (*Kanonier*) 1st Class	231
	Artilleryman (*Kanonier*) 2nd Class	462
	Artilleryman (*Kanonier*) 3rd Class	704
1 (Horse) Artillery Company (according to the Regulations of 14 Nay 1801)	Junior Captain (*Capitän*)	1
	Senior Lieutenant	1
	Junior Lieutenant	1
	Master Sergeant (*Oberfeuerwerker*)	2
	Senior NCO (*Wachtmeister*)	1
	Quartermaster Sergeant (*Furier*)	1
	Company Surgeon	1
	Senior Sergeant (*Feuerwerker*)	2
	NCO (*Unteroffizier*)	6
	Trumpeter	2
	Bombardier 1st Class	6
	Bombardier 2nd Class	6
	Artilleryman (*Kanonier*) 1st Class	18
	Artilleryman (*Kanonier*) 2nd Class (mounted)	54
	Artilleryman (*Kanonier*) 3rd Class (dismounted)	10
	Veterinarian (*Kurschmied*)	1
	Blacksmith farrier (*Fahnenschmied*)	1
	Saddler	1
	Wagon Maker (*Wagner*)	1
	Tack Master (*Schirrmeister*)	2
	Workman (*Knecht*)	48
	Workman in Reserve (*Knecht in Reserve*)	12
1 Worker (*Ouvrier*) Company (according to the Regulations of 25 March 1800)	Senior Captain (*Hauptmann*)	1
	Senior Lieutenant	1
	Junior Lieutenant	1
	Sergeant (*Feldwebel*)	1
	Quartermaster Sergeant (*Furier*)	1
	Corporal (*Korporal*)	5
	Vice Corporal (*Vize-Korporal*)	5
	Blacksmith (*Schmied*)	6
	Locksmith (*Schlosser*)	3
	Nail Maker (*Nagelschmied*)	1
	Driller (*Bohrer*)	2
	Gunsmith (*Büchsenmacher*)	6
	Wagon Maker (*Wagner*)	7
	Turner (*Drechsler*)	1
	Carpenter (*Zimmermann*)	4
	Joiner / Cabinet Maker (*Schreiner*)	4
	Drummer (*Tambour*)	1

---

31 The basic principle was formulated in March 1800: "For the defense of your Electoral Princely Majesty's state, 80 field pieces will suffice. Each piece will have 1 non-commissioned officer and 10 artillerymen, therefore, 880 men as crews for the number of cannon above. A captain can hardly preside over more than 8 guns, and an officer not oversee more than 2 cannon." (quoted from F. Münich, pages 277-278).

32 The Arsenal Main Directorate was responsible for the supervision of the various technical workshops and the design of new artillery piece and wagon models (F. Münich, page 291).

Each company served a battery. A cannon was crewed by 1 NCO and 10 *Kanoniere* (artillerymen), each howitzer was crewed by 1 *Feuerwerker* and 12 bombardiers.

The authorized number of horses for the horse artillery company was 113 riding horses (including the officers' horses), 64 draft and 24 pack horses. The five corporals of the *Ouvrier* Company were to be made up of 1 black-

Artillerymen on a "sausage wagon" ("*Wurstwagen*") after 1809
Extract from an engraving by J. L. Rugendas

smith, 1 driller, 1 gunsmith, 1 *Wagner* and 1 joiner or carpenter.

Per the decree of 14 May 1801, the mounted company had 6 six-pounder cannon and 2 seven-pounder howitzers. For the 1805 campaign, the number of guns per (foot) artillery company was set as 2 twelve-pounder and 8 six-pounder cannon and 2 seven-pounder howitzers; in addition there were the munition wagon as well as 1 field forge, 1 coal wagon and 1 supply wagon.

The Army Order of 24 September 1806 increased the Artillery Regiment to 4 battalions each with 4 companies. Each company was to include 100 men and serve a battery of 6 guns.[33]

On 21 June 1807, the Worker (*Ouvrier*) Company was removed from the Artillery Regiment and subordinated to the Arsenal Main Directorate (*Zeughaus-Hauptdirektion*).

On 28 September 1806, a command was issued creating the Artillery and Army Carriage (*Artillerie- und Armee-Fuhrwesen*) Battalion. This was composed of 8 companies and included 1 Senior Captain (*Hauptmann*) as the battalion commander, 1 quartermaster, 2 actuaries[34], 1 Senior Blacksmith, 9 lieutenants (including 1 Adjutant), 8 *Wachtmeister*, 8 *Furiers*, 32 corporals, 8 trumpeters, 16 blacksmiths, 16 saddlers and 960 privates. Additionally, for each pair of horses there was one driver (*Knecht*). Six companies were for transporting the artillery the forces' vehicles, two companies were subordinate to the General Commissariat and provide transportation for the army leadership, the administration and the medical service.

The Rescript (*Reskript*) of 29 April 1811 consolidated the various units into the Artillery Corps under which fell the Artillery Brigade, consisting of the Artillery Regiment and the Artillery- and Army Carriage Battalion, as

---

33 Xylander gives the total strength of the regiment as 1,634 men. The companies each included 1 Hauptmann or Kapitän, 1 senior lieutenant, 2 junior lieutenants, 1 Oberfeuerwerker, 1 Furier, 2 bombardier corporals, 6 Kanoniere corporals, 8 bombardiers 1st class, 8 bombardiers 2nd class, 16 Kanoniere 1st class, 16 Kanoniere 2nd class, 36 Kanoniere 3rd class and 2 drummers (1. Band, pages 367-368).

34 Schreiber.

well as the Arsenal Main Directorate with its subordinate Worker (*Ouvrier*) Company.

The Artillery Regiment still consisted of 4 battalions, but now with 5 companies, of them 1 light and 1 reserve company. Each company was to have 100 men. The Artillery Regiment's staff had 1 colonel/commandant, 4 lieutenant colonels, 4 majors, 5 adjutants, 4 *Junker*, 1 regimental quartermaster, 1 auditor, 1 regimental surgeon, 2 battalion quartermasters, 4 battalion surgeons, 4 surgeons' assistants, 1 regimental drummer, 2 battalion drummers and 1 provost.

The Artillery- and Army Carriage Battalion now formed 4 Divisions each with 2 companies. Its staff consisted of 1 lieutenant colonel as the commander, 1 major, 4 *Rittmeisters*, 1 adjutant, 1 battalion quartermaster, 1 battalion auditor, 1 battalion surgeon, 1 surgeon's assistant, 1 horse veterinarian (*Pferdearzt* - previously the senior blacksmith, *Oberschmied*), 4 division blacksmiths, 1 staff trumpeter, 1 wagon master (*Wagenmeister* - formerly *Geschirrmeister*), 1 master blacksmith (*Schmiedemeister*), 1 master saddler, 1 *Feuermeister*, 1 provost. The 8 companies had 8 senior lieutenants, 8 junior lieutenants, 8 1st *Wachtmeister* sergeants, 8 *Furiers*, 8 2nd *Wachtmeisters*, 48 corporals, 8 trumpeters, 16 blacksmiths, 16 saddlers, 1,072 soldiers as well as 80 riding horses and 640 draft horses.

The *Ouvrier* Company now had a strength of 100 men with 1 *Capitän*, 1 senior lieutenant, 2 junior lieutenants, 1 *Feldwebel*, 1 *Furier*, 6 sergeants, 6 corporals, 2 drummers, 20 workers (*Ouvriers*) 1st class and 60 workers 2nd class. There must have been 1 master gunsmith among the NCOs and 8 gunsmiths among the "*Ouvriers*".

After the Russia campaign, the Order of 6 March 1813 called for the re-raising of 20 artillery companies. For the Artillery- and Army Carriage Battalion, the 1st and 2nd Divisions were to be reestablished initially.

At the beginning of the 19th century, the Bavarian Army's artillery were primarily Austrian models.[35] By setting up a foundry in Augsburg as well as modifying the gun models, Lieutenant General Manson reduced the dependence on deliveries of guns from foreign sources.[36] After 1805, six-pounder and twelve-pounder cannon and seven-pounder howitzers were envisioned as the standard under Manson's system. The gun carriages were copied from the French Gribeauval system and fashioned completely of wood, with 1,72 diameter wheels. The gun carriage was on a limber that was equipped with a limber box. Equipment and ammunition could be carried in it and it could transport two soldiers.[37] By setting up a saltpeter refinery in the Munich Arsenal, the kingdom was able to produce gunpowder by itself.

Napoleon let the Bavarian army have two complete new Austrian "sausage batteries - *Wurstbatterien*[38] - from the stocks of the Viennese Arsenal which were used to convert two foot batteries to "traveling" ("*fahrende*") batteries.[39]

From the experiences with the Austrian "*Wurstbatterien*," which due to their length were not easy to aim, General Manson introduced Bavarian "*sausage wagons*" ("*Bayerische Wurstwagen*") in 1808.

In 1811, arsenals were located in Munich, Augsburg, Nurnberg, Innsbruck, Ingolstadt, Kufstein, Oberhaus, Rothenberg, Rosenbergand Lindau.

Lieutenant General Manson fostered the professionalizing of the Artillery Corps with the founding of an artillery school in which all Bavarian artillery senior and junior lieutenants would be trained.

The Pontooneer Corps (*Pontonier-Korps*) as created by orders issued on 17 September 1809. It was to consist of 2 companies each with 1 senior lieutenant, 2 junior lieutenants, 1 Senior Field Bridge Master (*Ober-Feld-Brückenmeister*), 2 Junior Bridge Masters (*Unter-Feld-Brückenmeister*), 6 corporals, 1 drummer, 20 Pontooniers 1st Class and 40 Pontooneers 2nd Class. The staff included 1 Field Bridge Director (*Feldbrückendirektor* – in the rank of Major), 1 Field Bridge Inspector (*Feldbrückeninspektor* in the rank of captian), 1 Adjutant and 1 scribe (*Schreiber*). After the 1809 campaign ended, the Corps was disbanded on 23 November 1809 before it reached its authorized strength.

Per an order on 11 March 1804, the Engineer Corps (*Ingenieurkorps*) was subordinated to the Quartermaster General and should the need arise, it could be put under General Staff services. It consisted of 1 colonel, 1 major, 3 captians, 3 senior lieutenants and 2 drivers. The 1811 Rank List (*Rangliste*) showed 1 major general (named d'Handel), 2 lieutenant colonels, 5 captians, 4 senior lieutenants and 8 junior lieutenants for the Engineer Corps.

---

35 *The production took place in the Munich Arsenal with support by civilian foundaries.*

36 *From 1802 to 1830, 128 six-pounder canon, 80 twelve -pounder canon, 4 one-pounder canon, 61 seven-pounder howitzers and 22 mortars of various calibers were produced in Bavaria.*

37 *The limbers' wheels had a diameter of 1,25 meters. There are extensive descriptions of the artillery material under Masons's system in Xylander's work (Volume 1, pages 296-298).*

38 *Long chests on the canon gun carriages could hold ammunition but also transport artillerymen quickly.*

39 *These two mounted batteries were employed in the war against Prussia and Russia at the end of 1806.*

Bavarian artillery in action 1809
Augsburger Bilderserie, Universität- und Landesbibliothek Darmstadt

The Recruit: entry on duty by a conscript about 1810
Colorized etching by Friedrich Campe, Nürnberg
in Anne S.K. Brown Military Collection, Providence, USA

The Farewell (*Der Abschied*)
Colorized engraving, Anne S.K. Brown Military
Collection, Providence, USA

Other Branches

On 8 August 1805, Maximilian Joseph converted the Military Academy to a Cadet Corps as the forge for cadre for the officer corps. A total of 210 cadets[40] at the age of 10 were to be admitted and trained over the course of eight years in the Cadet Corps.

At the beginning of the 19th century, the domestic law enforcement for the country was carried out by troops, who were recruited from the units located in the garrisons. However, the war of 1805 saw the need for the creation of a police watch (*Polizeiwache*) as well as a "Toll Patrol Corps" (*Maut-Patrouillen-Korps*), neither of which were under the military administration.[41] To put an end to the capriciousness of these police units, in 1812 a police force (*Gendarmerie*) was to be formed again under military authority. this unit was established by an edict of 11 October 1812[42] and was to take up its duties on January 1, 1813. A general was appointed as the senior commander, assisted by 1 adjutant, 1 auditor and 1 provost.

The *Gendarmerie* was to consist of 348 cavalrymen and 1,332 infantrymen. The mounted units were divided into three squadrons each divided into 16 "brigades" with one "*Brigadier*" and 6 soldiers. Each squadron was led by a captain (*Rittmeister*) who was joined by 3 Lieutenants, one First *Wachtmeister*, three Second *Wachtmeisters* and 16 "*Brigadiers*". The infantry was made up of 12 companies each with 12 "*brigades*" with 1 "*Brigadier* " and 8 soldiers. The company was under a captain (*Hauptmann*) who was authorized 2 lieutenants, 1 *Feldwebel*, 12 sergeants and 12 "*Brigadiers*". In situations where a squadron had to be pulled together, musicians from surrounding regiments were temporarily detailed to the *Gendarmerie*.

In the Kingdom of Bavaria, these Gendarme units were divided into three Legions[43] that were under the command of a senior officer who was supported by a quartermaster and an Adjutant.

Along with these police units, the so-called citizens' military (*Bürgermilitär*) were organized in the Bavarian communities per an order of 3 April 1807 that were to be dispersed throughout the entire country. The mission was primarily to secure the cities and communities in case of war, if the regular forces had to leave their garrisons. The organizing of the *Bürgermilitär* was the responsibility of the communities and was established with 1 junior lieutenant, 2 corporals and 1 drummer, so long as at least 20 men could be mustered. A *Bürgermilitär* company had to consist of at least 60 armed men, and four companies formed a battalion. One of the four companies was distinguished as the grenadier company. The battalion commander was a field grade officer (*Stabsoffizier*). Enlistment of musicians was permitted. In the event that at least 60 mounted men could be formed up, a squadron could be created. Creation of an artillery company was also authorized as long as adequate artillery pieces were available in a town.

Because the *Bürgermilitär* was exclusively concentrated in cities and towns, the mobilization for the 1809 campaign demonstrated the need for further measures for civil defense. The 6 April 1809 Instructions called for the creation of six battalions of four companies of National Guard (*Nationalgarde*). An additional Instruction on 6 July 1809 called for an extensive structuring of the National Guard. Three classes of the National Guard were established in this edict. The National Guard 1st Class should form a reserve for the field army[44], the National Guard 2nd Class should be employed as a national defense against internal and external enemies, and the National Guard 3rd Class should be used exclusively for maintaining domestic order.

For the National Guard 2nd Class a so-called Mobile Legion was to be set up in each of the kingdom's districts. The authorized strength of a Mobile Legion was from 4 to 8 battalions according to the size of the district. Each battalion had 4 companies. Each battalion was led by a major with a staff of 1 adjutant, 1 auditor, quartermaster, 1 surgeon and 1 assistant ("*Junker*"). A company should include 1 captain, 1 senior lieutenant, 2 junior lieutenants, 1 *Feldwebel*, 2 *Furiers*, 2 sergeants, 8 corporals, 1 bugler, 3 drummers, 10 privates first class (*Gefreite* – four of them with the sharpshooters), 26 sharpshooters and 120 militiamen. The companies were divided into four platoons and one sharpshooter detachment (*Schützenabteilung*)[45].

The National Guard 3rd Class was under civilian authorities and therefore included the *Bürgermilitär* described above.

Because of the Tyrolian Rebellion, King Maximilian Joseph issued an order of 7 May 1809, reactivating Mountain Sharpshooter Corps (*Gebirgsschützenkorps*) that had been decreed in 1805. This consisted of three detachments (*Abteilungen*)[46], the first was to have 500 men in service, while both the others were to have double that number ready as a reserve. Each detachment was to be divided into individual subordinate units each called

---

40 Among these 210 authorized positions were 100 with stipends, the remainder of the cadets had to pay a yearly fee of 204 guiders (F. Münich, p. 303).

41 They were overseen by regional state courts (Landgerichten)

42 The cavalry regiments had to give 348 experienced soldiers to the newly established Gendarmerie (F. Münich, page 265).

43 The 1st Legion was located in Munich and monitored the Isar River, the Inn River and the Salzach River District. The 2nd Legion, in Augsburg, took over this function for the Iller-, the Upper Danube and the Retzat District. The 3rd Legion was located in Regensburg and had oversight of the Main-, the Regen- and the Lower Danube District.

44 See also the designation of the line infantry's reserve battalions as National Guard 1st Class.

45 In the sharpshooter detachment (Schützenabteilung) of a company, 30 hand-picked men were to be enlisted who were practiced marksmen and who could be armed with rifles and/or sporting guns.

46 The 1st detachment was under the Traunstein Forest Inspection (Forstinspektion Traunstein), the 2nd under the Forstinspektion Rosenheim and the 3rd under Inspektion Garmisch.

a "*Rotte.*" A *Rotte* included 50 sharpshooters, led by 1 *Ober-Rottmeister* and 1 *Unter-Rottmeister*. Four *Rottes* then formed a captains troop (*Hauptmannschaft*) subordinate to a Senior Forester (*Oberförster*). A complete detachment (*Abteilung*) was commanded by a Forest Inspector (*Forstinspektor*) who was to be supplied with an experienced officer for the troops. The first *Gebirgsschützenkorps* soldiers could be released from service as early as 10 June 1809.

Due to the extensive mobilization measures after the Russia campaign, the king promised the National Guard 2nd Class that it would exclusively be employed inside the kingdom. With the regulations of 28 February 1813, the battalions of the Mobile Legions now included 4 companies, each with 4 officers, 1 *Feldwebel*, 2 sergeants, 6 corporals, 2 drummers, 10 *Gefreiters* and 140 National Guardsmen. Included within the *Gefreiters* and National Guardsmen were a total of 20 sharpshooters (*Schützen*).

On 26 March 1813, King Maximilian Joseph ordered the creation of a mounted unit in the National Guard 2nd Class. With the Army Order of 1 April 1813 the creation of this regiment - with the name *National-Chevaulegers-Regiment* - was approved.[47] The regiment was to consist of 2 squadrons with 1 *Rittmeister*, 1 senior lieutenant, 2 junior lieutenants, 1 *Wachtmeister*, 1 *Furier*, 2 sergeants, 6 corporals, 2 trumpeters, 1 blacksmith, 1 saddler, 10 *Gefreiters* and 110 Chevaulegers. A squadron was authorized 134 horses.[48]

Some of the units in the National Guard 2nd Class requested the king also employ them outside the kingdom, notably the 3rd Battalion of the Upper Danube District (*Oberdonau-Kreis*) Mobile Legion on 7 August 1813 and the Prinz Carl *National-Chevaulegers-Regiment* on 12 August 1813. In recognition of this request, the infantry battalion received an infantry regiment model standard. The 3rd Battalion of the Oberdonau-Kreis Mobile Legion was renamed as the 1st National Field Battalion Augsburg (*1. National-Feld-Battalion Augsburg*), the National-Chevauleges were renamed the 7th Chevaulegers-Regiment Prinz Carl. More Infantry battalions of the Mobile Legions followed this example and were likewise converted to National Field Battalions. The following table lists the migration of all the battalions in their order up through October 1813:

---

47 Prinz Carl of Bavaria became the commander and the regiment accepted volunteers between the ages of 20 and 40.

48 Each squadron consisted of 4 platoons each with 12 Rottes and a skirmisher platoon. Two corporals, 4 Gefreite and 20 of the most experienced Chevaulegers were assigned to this platoon of skirmishers.

3rd Battalion Mobile Legion Oberdonaukreis	1st National-Feld-Bataillon Augsburg
3rd Battalion Mobile Legion Retzatkreis	2nd National-Feld-Bataillon Ansbach
2nd Battalion Mobile Legion Regenkreis	3rd National-Feld-Bataillon Amberg
2nd Battalion Mobile Legion Salzachkreis	4th National-Feld-Bataillon Salzburg
1st Battalion Mobile Legion Isarkreis	5th National-Feld-Bataillon München
2nd Battalion Mobile Legion Illerkreis	6th National-Feld-Bataillon Lindau
2nd Battalion Mobile Legion Isarkreis	7th National-Feld-Bataillon Landshut
3rd Battalion Mobile Legion Isarkreis	8th National-Feld-Bataillon München
1st Battalion Mobile Legion Regenkreis	9th National-Feld-Bataillon Regensburg
1st Battalion Mobile Legion Oberdonaukreis	10th National-Feld-Bataillon Augsburg
2nd Battalion Mobile Legion Oberdonaukreis	11th National-Feld-Bataillon Ingolstadt
4th Battalion Mobile Legion Regenkreis	12th National-Feld-Bataillon Amberg
1st Battalion Mobile Legion Innkreis	13th National-Feld-Bataillon Innsbruck
1st Battalion Mobile Legion Retzatkreis	14th National-Feld-Bataillon Ansbach
1st Battalion Mobile Legion Mainkreis	15th National-Feld-Bataillon Bayreuth
1st Battalion Mobile Legion Illerkreis	16th National-Feld-Bataillon Kempten
4th Battalion Mobile Legion Retzatkreis	17th National-Feld-Bataillon Nürnberg
4th Battalion Mobile Legion Isarkreis	18th National-Feld-Bataillon Landshut
4th Battalion Mobile Legion Unterdonaukreis	19th National-Feld-Bataillon Passau
3rd Battalion Mobile Legion Regenkreis	20th National-Feld-Bataillon Regensburg

Translator's Note: The Mobile Legions were based on districts (Kreise) which were named after rivers, e.g., Isar or Salzach, while the National Field Battalions were designated by the city or town in which they were headquartered, e.g., Amberg or Kempten. This table has retained the German river and place names.

UNIFORMS

Introduction

In March 1789, the system for uniforms was drastically reorganized and a radical change occurred in the appearance for all regiments in that a "common uniform" ("*Einheitsuniform*") was introduced for all the branches. The initiator was Sir Benjamin Thompson, *Graf* (Count) Rumford[49], who introduced, with his instructions, what was for that time an independent, progressive and economical regimen. He thus introduced lasting changes to the appearance of the army, so the basic color for the infantry and heavy cavalry – dragoons and cuirassiers - became white, and for the light troops and the Chevaulegers it became dark green.

In 1799 both the jaeger infantry (*Fußjäger*) regiments were converted to four independent light battalions which now switched to light green coats with black distinctions.

The uniforms and their patterns were, however, unpopular in the army during the entire period they were worn.

So in 1799-1800 the basic color of the coat, which had become a „*Kollet*," again became cornflower blue (*kornblumenblau*), which corresponds to what today would be called medium blue. The cut of the uniform returned to a more traditional pattern with an open lapels and long tails. The lower and more comfortable „*Rumford-Kasket*" was replaced by a tall leather helmet - the caterpillar helmet („*Raupenhelm*") that would remain the characteristic feature of Bavarian troops for over 80 years.

The next changes took place starting 1805-06, that remained until 1808 with only minor changes, then from 1809 to 1814 followed fashion aspects of that period. So the French influences also appeared in individual areas in the Bavarian Army uniforms that usually followed a more independent development. Certainly the desires of the King, as the commander-in-chief, and the economic need to minimize costs, caused one to constantly strive for simplicity and standardization. In contrast, the officers' urge to evade the rules and come up with their own styles is evident again and again.

Up to 1814 the regiments and battalions were differentiated by varying color distinctions and button colors. After 1814, the infantry regiments and the Chevaulegers all received the same red distinctions and were only recognizable by the numbers on their buttons.

Among the standard works that are indispensable for a basic understanding of the army's uniforms, the work by Müller-Braun[50], which describes in detail all the pieces of equipment and changes for the various branches, stands out.

Additionally, the *Rang und Stammliste von 1811*[51], the only contemporary written source of the Napoleonic era, provides information. Similarly one can find useful information and reference sources in the mostly very detailed regimental histories for the army that give considerable additional information on the development of the uniforms of the individual branches. Also the occasional contemporary pictorial depictions show interesting details – such as the plates in the *Augsburger Bilder*[52], the series by Weiland[53] and individual pictures in French series[54]. The paintings by Hess and Albrecht Adam in the „battle gallery" (*Schlachtengalerie*) in the Residence in Munich give a variety of information. But here one has to consider that some of the depictions were done after the Napoleonic era and later influences are evident in the uniforms.

Rank Insignia

Starting in 1802, a new and for that time unusual rank system was introduced in the Bavarian Army which was visibly distinguished by horizontal laces sewn on the collars. the laces' color was based on the color of the buttons of the respective regiment.

Junior Lieutenant	one narrow lace
Senior Lieutenant	two narrow laces
Captain (*Hauptmann/Rittmeister*)	three narrow laces

The staff/senior officers had an additional collar edging of gold or silver lace with:

Major	one narrow lace
Lieutenant Colonel	two narrow laces
Colonel	three narrow laces

General Officers and Staff

Adjutant General (General-Adjudant) and Aide-de-Camp (Flügel-Adjudant) of the King[55]

The headgear was the bicorn with a blue and white feather support and white plumage. On the edge of the hat was a broad bordering.

---

49 Sir Benjamin Thompson, born 1753, an emigre from the United States, was named by King Max-Joseph to be the Minister of War and Bavarian Adjutant General and raised to the nobility as Count (Graf) von Rumford in recognition of his services. In 1799 his influence waned. He died in 1814 in Paris.

50 See bibliography; English title would would be „The Organization, Clothing and Equipment of the Royal Bavarian Army 1806-1906"

51 See the bibliography; English title would be "The Rank and Origin List of 1811."

52 Predominantly showing European military uniforms, series published ca. 1800-1810.

53 C.F. Weiland, Charakteristische Darstellung der k.u.k. Französischen Armee und iherer Alliierten 1812.

54 Martinet, Basset, Genty.

55 General-Adjutants General held the rank of a general, officers up to the rank of General were called „Flügel-Adjutanten [plural] (aides-de-camp). In 1811 the king had four each Adjutants General and Flügel-Adjutanten at his disposal.

Generals and General Staff
Upper row: **collar insignia (General (1811), Lieutenant General, Major General), Lieutenant General in mounted gala uniform,**
general's gala dress coat, General in gala dress, Major General in campaign coat.
Lower row: **Artillery General, Infantry Adjutant General, Major in the General Staff in gala uniform, Captain in the General Staff in frock coat, Cavalry Lieutenant Colonel in the General Staff in gala dress.**

Cornflower blue coat with red collar, facings and cuffs and coattail turnbacks. Seven horizontal loops on the facings, four more on the cuffs. Close-fitting white breeches. Aiguillettes on the right shoulder. Around the waist, a silver sash worked through with blue silk thread.

Broad gray trousers with a red stripe down the leg and buttons to close them were worn in the field.

Rectangular red cloth shabraque and holster covers with a broad solver border with an additional fringe on the edge.

The Cavalry

The bordering on the hat, lace and button color were silver. White vest; saber as weapon.

The Infantry

As above, but in gold. Yellow vest; sword as weapon.

Generals Commanding Troops or the Proprietor of a Regiment

The headgear consisted a tall black felt bicorn. The upper edge of both brims were bordered with a 9.5 cm (3¾ inch) wide silver lace. The lace had a rounded serrated edge. Along the border was white plumage from ostrich feathers. On the right front side an eight-pointed star was attached with a silver loop and cockade. After 16 February 1806, a blue and white cockade. At each end of the hat was a silver tassel.

Starting on 27 April 1804, the bicorn was worn fore and aft. On campaign the hat was worn side to side. To secure it better in strong winds, bad storms or while riding, a black silk ribbon or a black leather strap was tied under the chin.

After December 1805 the queue was abolished and the hair was worn short.

Since 1799 the generals again wore a cornflower/medium blue coat of a frock pattern with red collar, lapels/facings, cuffs and coattail turn-backs. By an order in March 1803, a 3 cm (1 ¼″) wide embroidery long lace of small laurel branches with intertwined ribbons was introduced that was attached to the collar, facings and cuffs. It was also added to the the coat pockets on the coattails and their turn-backs.

The cut of the coat was fixed with the April 1804 regulations and renewed in September 1807. Until then, the lapels/facings were closed down to the navel and the coattails reached to the hollow of the knee. From 1811 they were closed down to the hips.

On each facing, seven embroidered button loops flaps, and embroidery on the sides at the waist.

On the coattails two each and two more on the cuff flaps, and on the pocket flaps and between the buttons at the waist.

Buttons were silver-plated.

White vest closed in the front with a single row of ten buttons.

On both sides were pocket flaps with curved lower edges. Close fitting cloth pants with heavy cavalry boots.

Generals, who at the same time were sponsors of regiments were free to wear the uniform of their unit/regiment with embroidery on the collar according to their rank.

From August 1804 white leather gloves. Mounted generals wore cuffed gloves of the style worn by the light cavalry.

The sash was 12 cm (3¾″) wide with four blue silk stripes interwoven. At its ends were two tassels with approximately 13 cm (5 1/8″) long fringes. They remained the rank distinction for general officers until after 1812.

The sword for infantry generals with a 2.5 cm (1″) wide silver sword strap that was worked through with 4 light blue silk threads and had a tassel at the end. Cavalry generals had sabers.

Lieutenant General (General-Lieutenant or Divisionaer)

All parts of the uniform that were in the distinction color were decorated with broad, heavy silver embroidery. Loops on the facings, pockets and waist.

Major General (General-Major or Brigadier)

Simple embroidery on the collar and cuffs. From 1812 on, the sash was no longer worn for the gala uniform.

Campaign Uniform (Felduniform):

Starting in February 1808, the generals were allowed to wear black bicorn hats without bordering and with black plumage for daily and undress duty. The hat was worn from side to side for this uniform.

Starting in January 1804, the coats were introduced for daily use or for campaign. In this case, the embroidery was only visible on the collar; and the other reduced embroidery on the coat was hidden.

The lapels were folded over one another so that the embroidery was hidden and only the red lining was visible at the seam.

Original pieces[56] like both Prince Ludwig's and General Wrede's 1809 campaign coats show differing embroidery or its absence on the lapels so that one can conclude that the cut and embellishments were very individualized.

Sleeved Overcoat (*Aermelmantel* or *Roquelor*). Starting in October 1803, it was made of light gray cloth and had a standing collar of gray velvet. The cape portion reached to the elbows. The overcoat was closed by two rows each of six metal buttons.

---

56   Bayerisches Armeemuseum (Bavarian Army Museum), Ingolstadt

From left to right: NCO of the mounted artillery 1813-14 according to Roger Forthoffer; grenadier Regt. Preysing in the field uniform 1807 to 1812 per J. Arnold; second-lieutenant of Chevauleger Regt. Kronprinz 1812, per Neumann.
Plate by Patrice Courcelle, in the collection of Markus Gaertner

Generals of the Royal Suite (Generale a la Suite)
Bicorn without a bordering.
Coat with black velvet facings, collar, cuffs and turnbacks. White vest. Silver-plated buttons.

Artillery Generals
Bicorn had white feather trim.
Dark blue coat with black red-edged facings. Scarlet red cuffs and collar with gold embroidery. Red coat and coattail lining. Scaled epaulets on both shoulders. Gilt buttons. The embroidery was also gilt. Silver sashes. Dark blue close-fitting pants with bucket top boots.

Engineer Generals (General der Ingenieure)
Same uniform as for the artillery however, all embroidery and buttons were in silver. Also scaled epaulets on both shoulders.
Shabraque was of red cloth with a simple silver border that had silver bullions (tassels) and along which was silver embroidery in the shape of laurel branches. In the pointy end there was the royal monogram in gold stitching that was also surrounded by laurel branches. Pistol holsters also decorated with border stitching.

Gendarmerie General ("Charge" as Chief of the Corps from 11 October 1812)
"Steel green" (*"stahlgrüner"*) coat with red facings, cuffs and collar with gold stitching. Lining at the waist was dark green, gilt buttons and scale epaulets. Dark green pants with red piping along the sides.

Quartermaster General of the Staff (General- Quartiermeister Stab):
Bicorn with a simple, broad lace and a star-shaped cockade below the national cockade, and a white and blue hanging feather plume. For cavalry officers the hat had no border however it had a white and blue erect plume.
Cornflower blue coat of the same cut as for general officers, however, with dark blue velvet insignia on the collar, the facings, the latter decorated with seven silver laces and tassels. The facings were piped in red. Below each of the facings were two more laces. Four laces on the cuffs and two more on the buttons in the back at the waist. Coat lining and piping were in red. Silver-plated buttons.
Silver epaulets. White vest. White pants, but yellowish for the cavalry with high bucket top boots.
As rank insignia, the sash was also worn starting in 1812.
The undress coat was as described above, however it had only one row of buttons and no coattail pockets.

Shabraques were cornflower blue with a silver border and tassels. In the corners the royal monogram surrounded by laurel branches was embroidered in gilt.

Generals' Adjutants.
Sash worn over the shoulder, otherwise they wore the same uniform as their unit.

Generals as Commandants of a Fortress or City:
Bicorn with broad curved silver braid as its bordering.
Cornflower blue coat with like-colored lining. The facings were of black velvet, as were the cuffs. No embroidery on the colored distinctions. Collar red with white piping. White vest and pants.

Field Jaeger Corps (*Feldjägerkorps*) – 1805 to 1808

This small corps consisted of mounted and foot jaegers.
As headgear they wore the bicorn with a plume. Green coat with long tails and yellow distinctions. Brass epaulets. Pants in the same color as the coat with yellow stripes down the sides. Black leather equipment with sabretache and saber.
The shabraque was like that of the Chevaulegers, however with a green case for the overcoat.
The foot jaegers (*Jäger zu Fuß*) wore the coat with short tails, and the pants were worn with gaiters. They were to be armed with carbines and artillery model sabers.

Cadet Corps (*Kadetten-Korps*)

The *"Kaskett"* helmet as headgear. The single-breasted *"Kollet"* coat made of cornflower blue cloth. Black tabs on the collar and cuff flaps. Red piping on the breast seam and at the bottom of coat at the waist. White metal buttons. White vest. Gray trousers worn in black gaiters. For inclement weather a gray overcoat.
The cadet standard bearer (*Fahnen-Kadett*) wore the Kaskett with a bearskin caterpillar.

Officers
Bicorn with a wide curved silver braid as the border.
Coat with facings; black velvet as the insignia color. Coat with long red tails. White trousers worn in Hungarian boots. As armament they had a sword with a sword knot.

Hartschiere Court Guard-Body Guard
(Hofgarde-Leibgarde der Hartschiere)

Service Uniform

Tall bicorn with a silver border and a white hanging feather plume whose end transitioned to blue. Coat of cornflower blue cloth with long tails and black velvet collar, cuffs and facings. Wide silver lace on the collar, facings and the cuff flaps.

The coat turn-backs were buff colored edged in solver. White vest. Beige pants and lining. High bucket top boots with spurs.

Sword belt made of leather faced with black velvet edged in silver. The cartridge box and carbine bandolier were done in the same manner.

Gala Uniform

A light blue overcoat with black velvet stripes, the so-called *"Casaque"* with buff colored lining. Also buff colored knee-length pants with white stockings and shoes with buckles. As "armament," along with the sword they had a halberd.

Officers had silver fringed epaulets and sashes.

INFANTRY

Infantry of the Line

The *"Kaskett"* helmet was introduced from the end of 1799 to June 1800. It was commonly referred to as a *"Raupenhelm"* or caterpillar helmet and was the characteristic headgear of Bavarian forces starting with the Napoleonic era. The helmet consisted of an up to 30 cm (12") high bell-shaped body[57] of black lacquered leather. A black woolen caterpillar crest was attached down the center of the body from the nape to half way to the front of the dome. This comb was initially made of hair, however was filled with hay or straw so that it formed a leather "sausage" that was enclosed with black similarly shaped fringes and tufts or with black lamb's wool. The body could be adjusted to individual needs by means of a strap and buckle on the lower edge. On the front side was a visor was attached to protect from light or effects of the sun. In the rear sometimes a neck visor was individually attached although it was not according to regulation.[58] But it protected the neck from rain. On the front side an oval brass plate was attached that had the royal "MJ" monogram (from 1800 to 1806 electoral principality) and "MJK" (from 1806 to 1815), decorated with the crown on top.

The lower rim of the helmet was equipped with a brass band. A thin chain ran along each side from the plate and was attached to the side with a retaining button.

Cross of the Military-Max-Joseph Order
(*Kreuz des Militaer*-Max-Joseph-Ordens)
(from Perrot, 1821)

The chinstraps were made of black leather and attached at the top with a smooth disk. The straps themselves were covered with a so-called "armored small chain" (*"Panzerkettchen"*) of brass. The cockade - white-light blue-white – was attached on the left side over the chinstrap disk from 21 January 1806 onward.

Additionally for the elite and fusilier companies there was a *Huppette* – a truncated tapered socket above the cockade on the left side for the elite's distinction or the fusilier's pompom.

The *Kaskett* with a weight of about 1.5 kilograms or 3 ⅓ pounds and previously described height, had a high center of gravity and was therefore unstable on one's head and was difficult to keep on during abrupt move-

---

57 They were also called "Kasten." The models had a number of variants whose height and shape differed. Moreover, until 1823, the helmet was the soldiers' property and they were responsible for its maintenance and care.

58 Various forms of or the absence of visors are depicted.

Regimental Distinction Colors, 1805-1806		
Regiment	Distinction Color	Button color
Leibregiment	red 7 white laces on the facings	white metal
Kurprinz	red 7 yellow laces on the facings	yellow metal
Herzog Carl	red	yellow metal
Von Preysing	rose (pink) with red piping	white metal
Herzog Wilhelm	scarlet red	white metal
Herzog Pius	yellow	yellow metal
Graf Ysenburg	scarlet red	yellow metal
Junker	crimson	white metal
Von Kinkel	orange	yellow metal

Regimental Distinction Colors, 1806[59]-1814				
Regiment	Facings	Collar	Piping / Laces	Button Color
1. König	red	red	white Litzen	white metal
2. Kronprinz	red	red	yellow Litzen	yellow metal
3. Prinz Karl	red	red	white	yellow metal
4. Sachsen-Hildburghausen	yellow	yellow	red	white metal
5. von Preysing	rose (pink)	rose (pink)		white metal
6. Herzog Wilhelm	red	red	white	white metal
7. Löwenstein-Wertheim	rose (pink)	rose (pink)		yellow metal
8. Herzog Pius	yellow	yellow	red	yellow metal
9. Graf von Ysenburg	yellow	red	red	yellow metal
10. Junker	yellow	red	red	white metal
11a von Kinkel 1807-1811	green	red	red	white metal
11b von Kinkel starting in 1811	black	red	red	white metal
13. no title/name	black	red	red	white metal
Transferred to Berg in 1806, re-established in 1807, disbanded in 1811				
14. no title/name	black	red	red	yellow metal

59 After 1810 the regiments named after the Colonel-in-Chief. The 12th Regiment was disbanded.

Infantry Coat Schemes

Top row: 1st Infantry-Leibregiment (1811: 1st Infantry Regiment Koenig), 2nd Infantry Regiment (Line Infantry Regiment - LIR) Kronprinz, 3rd LIR Prinz Karl, 4th LIR Sachsen-Hildburghausen
Middle row: 5th LIR Preysing, 6th LIR Herzog Wilhelm, 7th LIR Loewenstein, 8th LIR Herzog Pius
Bottom row: 9th LIR Graf von Isenburg, 10th LIR Junker, 11th LIR Kinkel (1807-1811), 13th LIR (1811: 11th LIR Kinkel), 14th LIR (1811: 13th LIR)

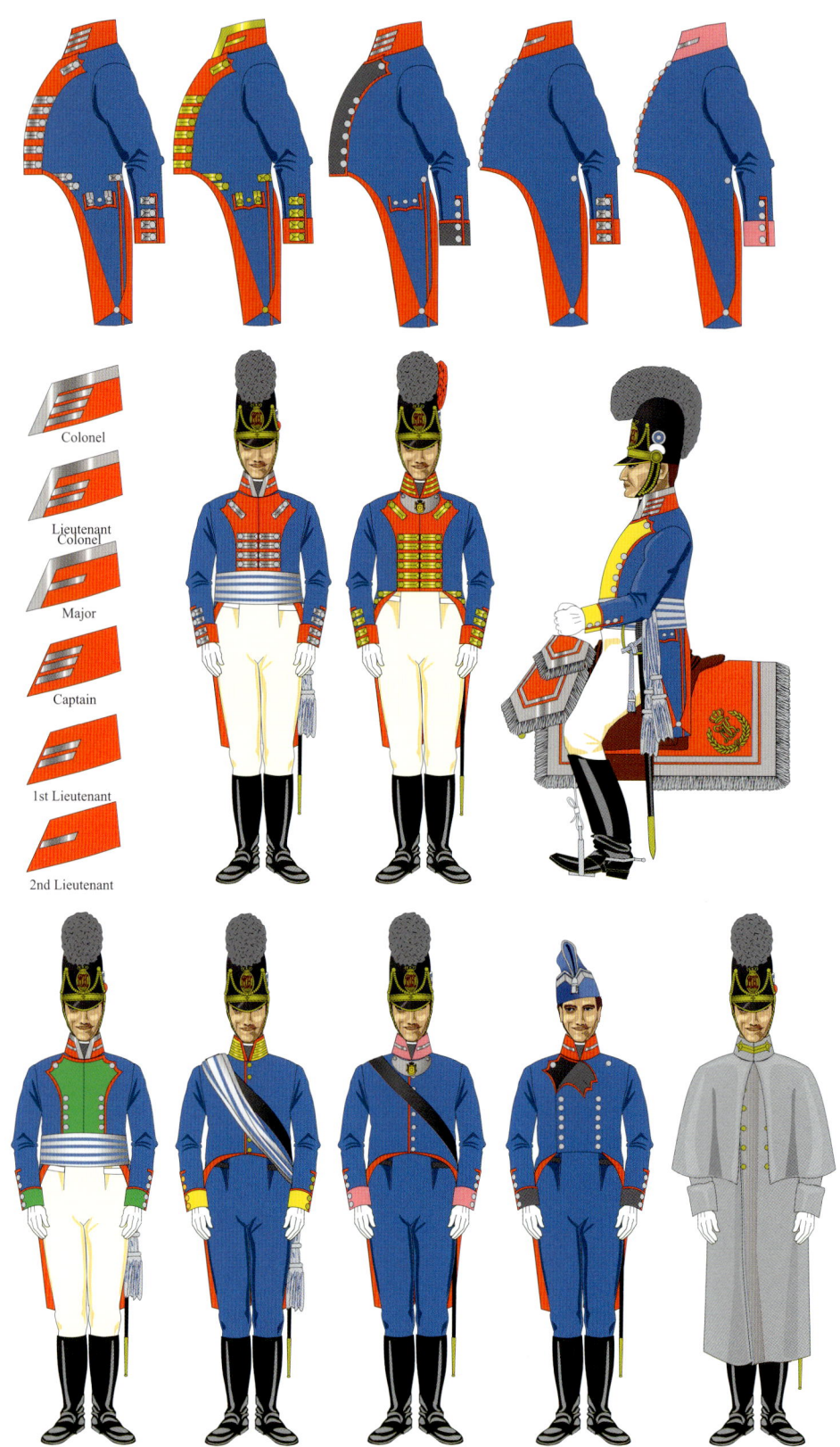

Infantry Officers

Top row: coat schemes (1st LIR Koenig, 2nd LIR Kronprinz, 13th LIR (1811: 11th LIR), frock coat 1st LIR Koenig, frock coat 5th LIR Preysing
Middle row: rank insignia (from top to bottom: colonel, lieutenant colonel, major, captain, first lieutenant, second lieutenant), major 1st LIR Koenig until 1812, captain 2nd LIR Kronprinz starting in 1812, colonel 10th LIR Junker mounted
Bottom row: major 11th LIR von Kinkel 1809-1811, captain 8th LIR Herzog Pius in frock coat as adjutant, second lieutenant 5th LIR Kinkel in frock coat, second lieutenant 13th LIR (1811: 11th LIR) with forage cap and buttoned back facings, officer in overcoat

Infantry Center Companies (*Zentrum-Kompanien*)

Top row: drummer 2nd LIR Kronprinz, fusilier 11th LIR Kinkel with equipment used until 1808, fusilier 5th LIR Preysing equipment used until 1808 rear view, fusilier 7th LIR Loewenstein with work pants used until 1808, fusilier 10th LIR Junker with forage cap and work pants
Bottom row: fusilier NCO 3rd LIR Prinz Karl, drummer 10th LIR Junker, fusilier 1st LIR Koenig in work pants with equipment starting in 1808, fusilier 9th LIR Isenburg with equipment starting in 1808 rear view, fusilier in an overcoat

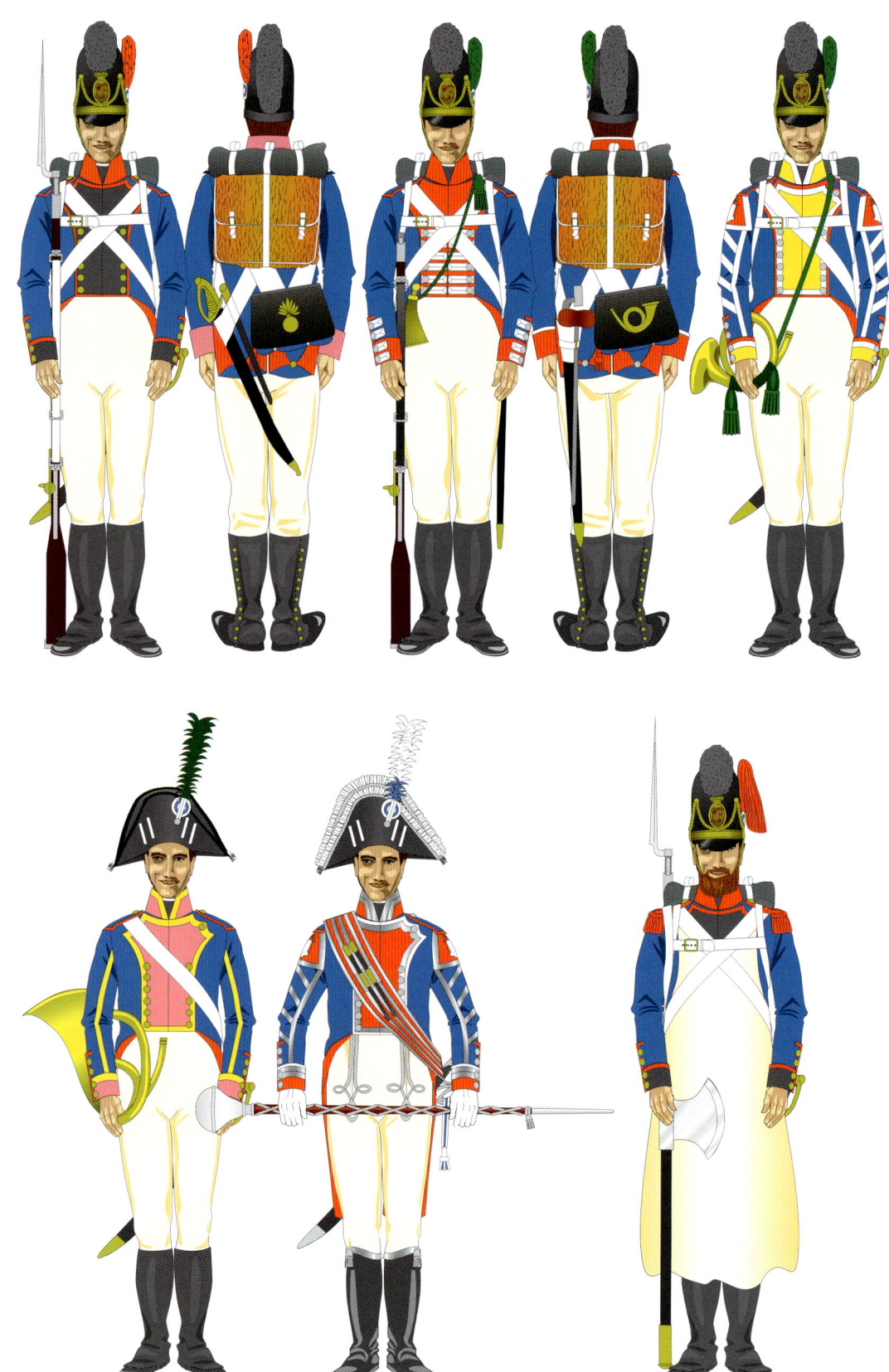

Infantry Elite Companies

Top row: grenadier 14th LIR (1811: 13th LIR) grenadier 7th LIR Loewenstein rear view, sharpshooter 1st LIR Koenig, sharpshooter 6th LIR Herzog Wilhelm rear view, bugler of the sharpshooters 4th LIR Sachsen-Hildburghausen starting 1811,
Bottom row: musician 7th LIR Loewenstein as bugler of the sharpshooters until 1811, drum major 3rd LIR Prinz Karl, sapper 14th LIR (1811: 13th LIR)

ments [60]. Additionally, precipitation or wind made it more difficult to wear.

The forage cap ("*Holzmütze*" or "*Lagermütze*") was cut in a pattern similar to the French "*bonnet de police*". The basic cloth was light blue with trim in the regimental color. The front of the cap was decorated with the company device, so the red grenade for the grenadiers, the green hunting horn for the sharpshooters, and the company number in the regimental color for the fusilier companies.

The cornflower blue coat was also introduced in 1800 and replaced the unpopular cut of the white "Rumford-Period" coat.

The facings were now closed to the waist, and a high collar and short coattails were added.

The cuffs were now in the distinction color. Above them was a vertical piping in the distinction color as a cuff flap; four buttons in the regimental color on the piping.

The facings, with seven buttons on each side, were worn closed. The buttons were flat, blank and slightly curved in the front.

The collar, cuffs and facings were in the regiment's distinction color, however, the coattail turnbacks were red for all regiments.

The shoulder straps were the same color as the coat and piped in red and attached with a button on the end by the collar.

Unique Features for Grenadiers, Sharpshooters and Fusiliers

The fusiliers wore these company insignia on the caterpillar helmet:

In the 1st battalion:
- 1st co. - white
- 2nd co. - white over yellow pompom
- 3rd co. - green
- 4th co. - green over white

In the 2nd battalion:
- 5th co. - red
- 6th co. - red over yellow
- 7th co. - blue
- 8th co. - blue over yellow

Starting April 1809, the grenadiers in the 1st battalion wore a red plume ("*Huppen*") and in the 2ns battalion a red over white plume. A grenade emblem was attached to the cartridge box lid.

After March 1804, the sharpshooters, as light companies in the 1st battalion had a green plume and in the 2nd battalion a green over white plume. They had a hunting horn emblem on the lid of their cartridge box.

For bad weather the plumes were covered with black or green waxed cloth.

The close-fitting white pants were worn stuck inside short black cloth gaiters that were closed on the sides with 12 small buttons For field duty, long reinforced white linen pants, called "*Arbeitshosen*" (work pants) used. Gray or blue pants are also depicted in some sources.

Every two men shared a small cooking crock or field pot (*Kochtopf* or *Feldkessel*)[61] and every 15 men shared a large pot that was carried in turns by attaching it to that man's pack.

Starting 5 November 1807, a backpack of calfskin was introduced that had two white shoulder straps that were secured by two straps across the chest. Starting 1809, the overcoat was rolled up and buckled to the top of the pack. The light gray overcoat, introduced in October 1802, of "*Loden*" cloth had a 7.3 cm (3") long cloth patch with the regiment's distinction color on both sides of the collar, this was attached by a button on the front side. It reached to the calves. Starting 1810, the overcoat color was changed to dark gray, however both models were authorized for wear until 1812.

Starting on 18 January 1810, they were carried on their backs, which had been done in the field unofficially since 1809. Up till then, worn on the right shoulder to the left hip.

Additionally a field canteen of sheet zinc (*Zinkblech*)[62], a linen bread bag with a carrying strap of the same material. The cartridge box was made of strong black leather and could hold 60 cartridges. The box in the cartridge box measured 24 cm (9½") long, 13 cm (5 1/8") tall und 7 cm (2¾") deep. The lid was 30 cm (12") long. On the left side was a leather strap to button onto the uniform, to prevent it from slipping. It was carried on a white leather bandolier[63] over the left shoulder and attached under the shoulder strap. For the grenadiers a brass grenade was attached to the lid.

In bad weather and in the winter months, brown mottled gloves with fingers, or often also blue mittens.

All soldiers wore a short curved infantry saber with a simple grip and hilt. Initially the Model 1794, which had a leather-wrapped grip, was carried. Starting 1808, the Model 1808 with a brass grip was widely issued; it was carried on a bandolier worn over the shoulder.

The sharpshooters carried the "*Haubajonett*" (cutting edged bayonet).

---

60 *Described as unofficial by contemporaries. It was difficult to keep it on one's head in mountainous terrain or when negotiating obstacles. Also in hot or cold temperatures the Kaskett did not have "user friendly" characteristics.*

61 *Called a "Kasserol" (casserole).*

62 *In peacetime maintained in the arsenal.*

63 *The bandolier was about 8-9 cm (3 1/8 – 3½") wide.*

NCOs

There were no rank distinctions attached to the coats. Insignia were the NCO's cane and the particular NCO's saber with strap and tassel of mixed white and blue wool. The master sergeants (*Feldwebel*) had their saber strap tassels of silver and blue silk and the officer's caterpillar crest on their helmets. White gloves with fingers.

Musicians - Drummers and Other Musicians

The companies each had two drummers and a fifer.

The musicians wore the same headgear and uniform as the troops. As a special means of recognition, they wore elaborate lace trim on the coat that was white or yellow corresponding to the regiment's metal button color. The arrangement of the trim was, according to the depictions, different depending on the regiment. For example, a v-shaped upward pointing chevron. The shoulders were decorated with so-called "swallows nests" in the regiment's color. The braiding was also in the color of the lace. The swallows nests were further decorated on the sides with the royal monogram on the coat of arms.

For Regiment No. 4, the lace on the sleeves consisted of only four diagonal bars that extended to the lace along the sleeve's seam.

For Regiment Ysenburg, No. 9, the drummer had no swallows nests but only the shoulder straps piped in red. Yellow lace edging on the collar in front and also an additional horizontal lace in yellow. Golden border on the facings.

For regiments No. 10, No. 11 and 13 it is indicated that the grenadier companies additionally wore red epaulets. Regiment. No. 11 instead of green had red swallows nests.

No. 13 is depicted with v-shaped chevrons pointing downward. Other variant show them pointing upward, however with red swallows nests, and with the royal monogram without the coat of arms.

The drum's shell was made of brass and the royal monogram and crown were embossed on the front side. The rims were made of wood and painted with alternating white and blue diagonal stripes. Drumsticks were black, and were stuck in the drum rims on the march. Fastenings and stretchers were made of white wool.

Fifers[64] carried their instrument in brass case over the shoulder.

Each regiment had a musical band whose members wore black bicorns. The coat was also trimmed with lace on the collar, facings and cuffs. The edging was either in silver or gold depending on the button color. For Regiment No. 13 additional edged sleeve seams have also been described.

Drummer-Major

Bicorn with edging in silver or gold corresponding to the button color, white plume with a blue base was added.

Edging braid also on the collar, facings and coattail turnbacks. Swallow's nests in the distinction color and enclosed with a braid. On both sleeves were v-shaped laces like for the drummers in silver or gold.

White close-fitting pants with Hungarian knotting and short Hungarian boots with trim and tassel in the button color.

The NCO's sabers were carried on a wide red bandolier with drumsticks at the chest level. The bandolier was edged on both sides with wide timed.

Drumsticks had silver-plated metal parts and cording.

Sappers, since 1804

Two senior privates (*Gefreite*) per company were chosen to be sappers. Ideally they were or had experience as woodcutters. They were to wear a heavy beard in the French fashion as the indicator of their status.

The uniform corresponded to those of the fusiliers with the following differences:

The *Kaskett* had a red drooping hair plume. Large white leather apron that hung around the neck and was tied around the hips. A crossed axes emblem made of wool was sewn on the left sleeve. On both shoulders were red woolen epaulets. The axe was carried in a white leather case on the shoulder.

A further indicator was the heavy engineer's axe (*Pionieraxt*) that had a special shape – wedge-shaped – for the Bavarian Army.

On the march, the sappers (also called *Pioniere*) carried the company guidon[65]. The musket was carried with a musket slung over the back.

Officers

The headgear remained the black bicorn until the end of 1805.

The *Kaskett* helmet was first officially introduced on 27 September 1805. The exception was for colonels who continued to wear the hat. All the metal fittings were gilded. The helmet's caterpillar was visibly larger and its exterior was of bearskin. The officers' scaled chinstrap was attached on the sides, as was the white and silver cockade, also called a *"Feldzeichen"*, literally a *"field sign"*.

The officers used the forage cap, even though unofficially.

The coats were the same pattern as for the troops, however, as a rule they were of better cloth and had long coattails reaching to the back of the knees. The coattails were adorned with diagonal pockets. For Regiments No. 1 and No. 2, the coat was additionally decorated with two

---

[64] From 1802 to 29 April 1811 the fifers were only assigned to the grenadier companies.

[65] See section on Flags and Company Guidons.

laces on each side at the bottom of the facings and on the coattail pockets. The buttons were silver plated or gilded.

From 1800 to 1812 the rank distinction was the sash of silver silk worked through with four light blue stripes. In March 1812, the gorget was introduced to replace the sash as the rank distinction. It was crescent-shaped like the French model and made of silver-plated steel. In the middle was the royal monogram on the gilded coat of arms, decorated with lions' heads.

Shortly before the campaign in Russia, in April 1812, an order was issued that the gorget should be covered with a light blue cloth when in the field. This was intended to avoid unnecessary casualties because the metal parts made the officers stand out and become like target disks ("*Zielscheibe*").

For the dress uniform they wore tight, white pants with Suvarov-Boots of black leather that were cut smoothly on the upper edges.

Starting in 1804, for the field or undress uniform, the officers wore a single-breasted, light blue frock coat with long coattails. Until February 1808, they wore gray and then afterwards light blue close-fitting pants.

Often, however, they also wore long pants in the same color, so in the 1st Regt. one wore long light blue trousers with red stripes on the sides.

Starting in 1803, the officers received a standard overcoat, the so-called "*Roquelaure*" that had a gray basic color and a wide cape over the shoulders.

Starting in 1805, it was allowed to carry the sword in a black polished belt worn over the shoulder. Because the sword was mostly privately acquired, there were various models of sword knots.

Shabraques for mounted and staff officers were poppy (*ponceau*) red with double silver/gilded border with fringes. In the rear corner was the gilded royal monogram with a crown and surrounded with laurels. Two pistol holster covers were similarly decorated.

For the adjutants, the shabraques and pistol holsters were without fringes.

Light Infantry Battalions

In general, the light infantry battalions' appearance corresponded to that of the infantry.

The *Kaskett* helmet was of the same model as described for the infantry. From 1803 to 1811, the company colors on the side of the helmet were:

1st company	white	
2nd company	green	
3rd company	red	fusilier company
4th company	blue	
5th company	yellow	depot company

The sharpshooter companies wore a green plume on the side.

The forage cap of green cloth with red piping was worn for casual duty. A green tassel was at the top of the cap.

The short-tailed coat was of light green cloth that was changed to dark green starting in 1809. All battalions had black facings and cuffs with red piping. The distinction color was visible on the collar and the button color. The coattails were red for all the battalions; the shoulder straps were green piped in red.

The pants were gray with close-fitting black gaiters. White "work pants" ("*Arbeitshosen*") were worn in the field and on camp duty.

Leather equipment was white. The carabineer company had a brass hunting horn emblem on the cartridge box cover. The sharpshooters additionally wore at their side a powder horn on a green woven cord with tassels.

Gray overcoat had a rectangular patch in the battalion color on the collar.

Distinction Colors 1806-1807

Battalion	Collar	Buttons
1st Habermann	red	white
2nd Ditfurth	red	yellow
3rd Preysind	black	yellow
4th Zoller/ 1807 Wreden	black	white
5th Dalwigk since 8/22/1806	red black	white
6th Taxis since 8/22/1806	red black	yellow

Distinction Colors 1808-1814

Battalion	Facings	Collar	Buttons
1st Gedoni	black	red	yellow metal
2nd Wrede	black	red	white metal
3rd Bernclau	black	black	white metal
4th Theobald	black	black	yellow metal
5th Buttler	black	yellow	white metal
6th La Roche	black	yellow	yellow metal

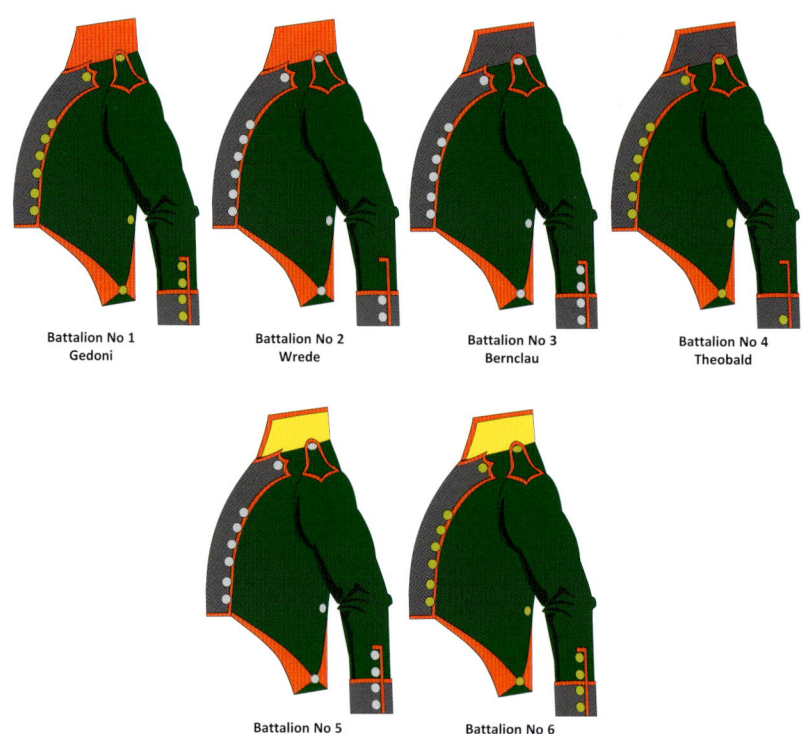

Light Infantry: Coat Schemes and Officers

Top row: coat schemes for 1st Battalion Gedoni, 2nd Battalion Wrede, 3rd Battalion Bernclau, 4th Battalion Theobald
Middle row: coat schemes for 5th Battalion Buttler, 6th Battalion LaRoche
Bottom row: major of 3rd Battalion Bernclau until 1812, major 4th Battalion Theobald starting 1812, second lieutenant of 5th Battalion Buttler in frock coat in the field, first lieutenant of 2nd Battalion Wrede with forage cap and folded over facings, officer in overcoat

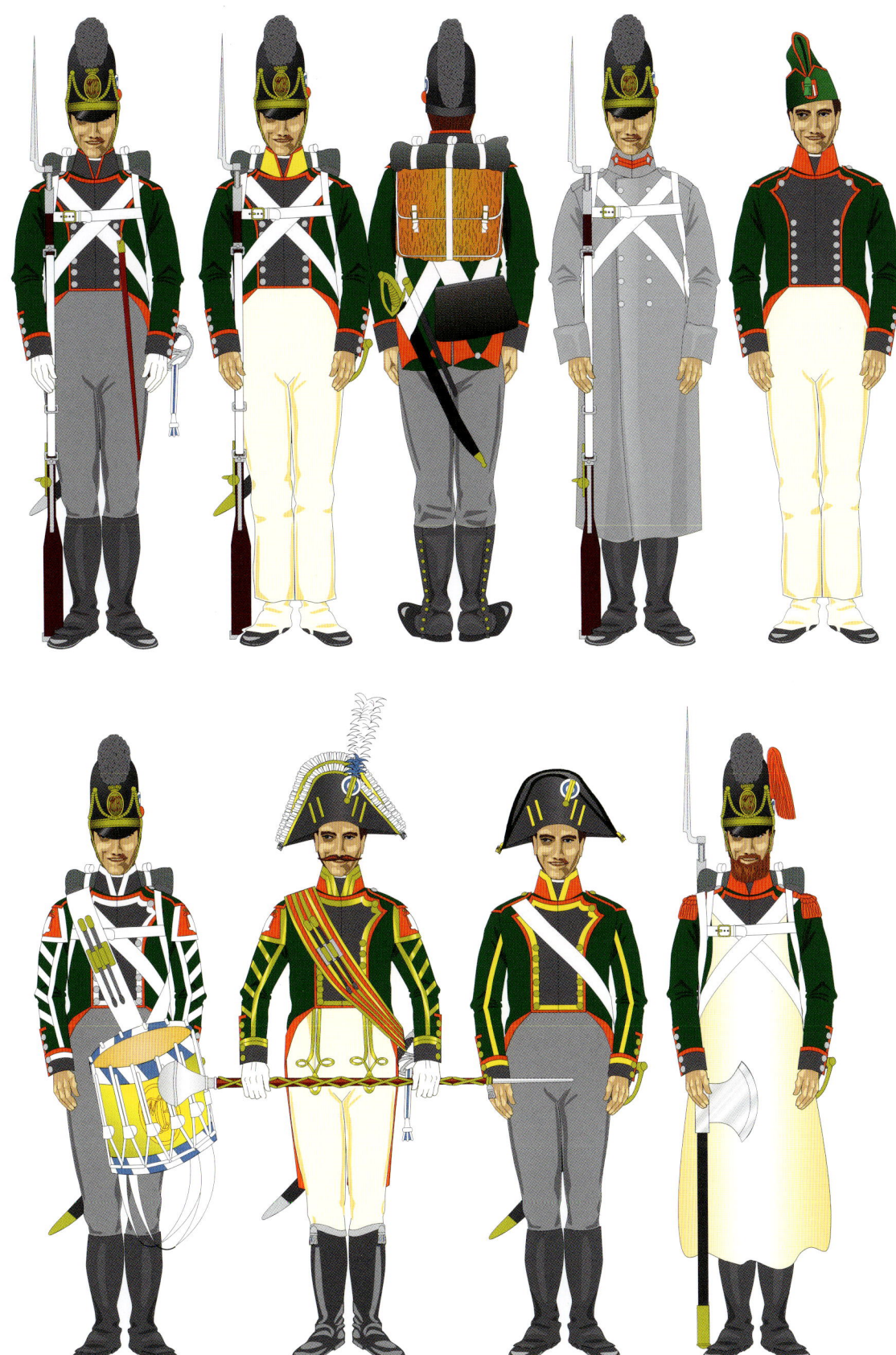

Light Infantry Center Companies

Top row: NCO of 2nd Battalion Wrede, fusilier of 5th Battalion Buttler in work pants, fusilier of 3rd Battalion Bernclau rear view, fusilier in overcoat, fusilier with forage cap, camp uniform
Lower row: Drummer of 3rd Battalion Bernclau, drum major of 1st Battalion Gedoni, musician of 1st Battalion Gedoni, sapper of 2nd Battalion Wrede

Light Infantry Elite Companies

Grenadier of 6th Battalion LaRoche, sharpshooter of 4th Battalion Theobald front and rear views, musician of 2nd Battalion Wrede as signalman for sharpshooters until 1811, bugler of 1st Battalion Gedoni starting 1811

Muskets and the infantry saber were the armament; for the carabiniers the saber had a 3 cm (1¼ in.) longer blade. The sharpshooters carried a 63.5 cm (25 in.) long cutting-edged bayonet (*Haubajonett*) instead of the saber. The ramrod was also attached in the bayonet scabbard, on the end of which was attached a wooden hammer for dislodging rounds stuck in the rifle's barrel.

NCOs
They wore the enlisted soldiers' style coat, but carried a cane and had a saber with a basket hand-guard as rank insignia.

Drummers/Buglers
Even though they were designated as light infantry, the battalions also had drummers who had rich lace on their collar, facings and sleeves to distinguish them. The color of the lace trim was oriented to the white or yellow button color. The swallows nests were red for all, with colored lace.

Starting in 1811, buglers were in use for the sharpshooters. They wore the same coat as the drummers. The signal horn was made of brass and had light green cords.

Drum Major/Battalion Drummer
Like for the infantry with lace trim on the distinctions (collar, etc.) and sleeves.

Musicians
They wore bicorns, long-tailed coats, also with edging.
Until 1811 two musicians with the sharpshooters served as signalmen and wore a green plume on their hat as an insignia.

Sapper/Pionier
Uniform distinctions and equipment like for the infantry.

Officers
Uniform pattern was like for the infantry.
The officers wore white pants for parades. However, for daily duty, in the field, and when wearing the frock coat, as a rule they wore long green pants. For the casual uniform, the single-breasted frock coat was worn with a black sword bandolier over the shoulder.

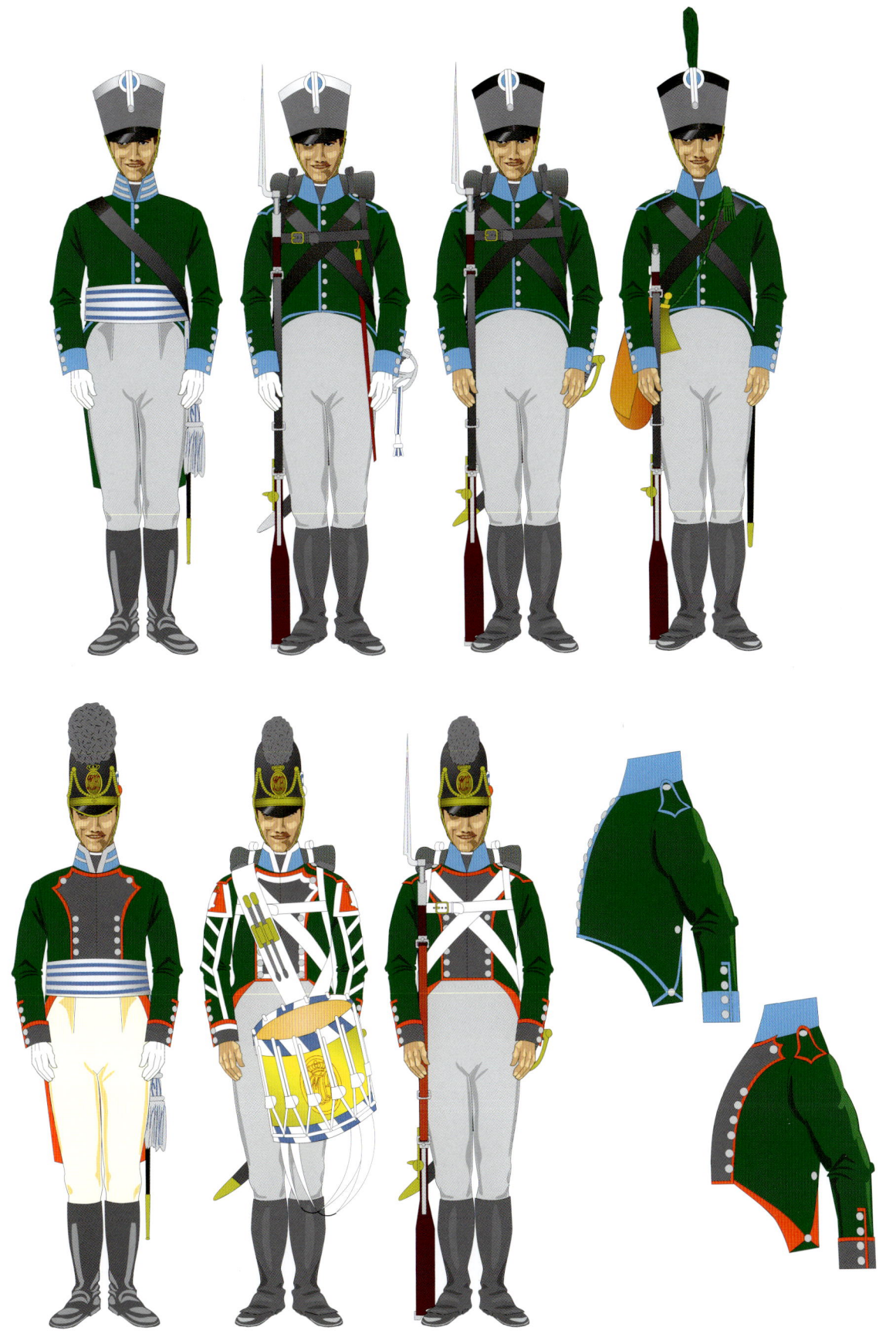

Tyrolean Jaeger Battalion (*Tiroler Jäger-Bataillon*) / Light Battalion Guenter

Top row: Tyrolean Jaeger Battalion: officer, NCO, jaeger, sharpshooter
Bottom row: Light Battalion Günter: officer, drummer, fusilier, Tyrolean Sharpshooters-Battalion coat, Light Battalion Günter coat

Tyrolean Jaeger Battalion

In 1807, the Tyrolean Jaeger Battalion was formed with volunteers from the new province. In 1811, it was designated Battalion No. 7 of the light infantry, however, it was disbanded that same year.

There were deviations in its uniforms from the rest of the army, e.g., its headgear was a shako with the Bavarian cockade on the front.

The sharpshooters wore an additional green plume on the shako.

Single breasted green coat with light blue distinctions on the collar, on the cuffs and piping on the coattails. Buttons were made of white metal. Leather equipment was black.

Instead of the backpack, the sharpshooters wore a "rifle satchel" ("*Buechsenranzen*") on their right side.

As the 7th Battalion uniform was made more like that of the light battalions, they received the caterpillar helmet as well as black facings with piping, but kept the light blue distinction color.

NCOs had white braid on the shako's upper rim.

Officers wore only the single-breasted frock coat. The shako rim had a silver braid, and for senior officers a double braid.

Garrison Troops

The *Kaskett* helmet was like that for the infantry. Single-breasted dark blue coat with white collar, cuffs and piping. Buttons of white metal. Gray vest and pants with black gaiters.

Dark blue forage cap with white piping and a tassel in front.

Weapons and leather equipment like for the infantry.

NCOs carried the steel basket-hilt saber

Officers

The bicorn with a silver loop with the cockade as the headgear. Long dark blue coat without lapels, with light blue lining and coattail turnbacks. White collar. Yellow vest and white trousers. The sword was worn on a black leather belt. Until 1812, the sash, and then also the gorget were the rank distinction.

CAVALRY

The headgear for the cavalry was, like for the infantry, the caterpillar helmet (*Kaskett* or *Raupenhelm*) with a few different details. For example, brass protective stiffeners ran vertically over the helmet from one retaining button to the other and one diagonally to the back for additional strength so forming a "V." A tall white plume was added to the left side. On the bottom of the front was a band of brass with the regiment's title, e.g., DRAGONER REGIMENT or CHEVLEGERS REGIMENT. The spelling was used for symetry. The rosette of course appeared in the middle of the helmet. The caterpillar for the troopers was thinner, like for the infantry, than for the officers and NCOs.

On the side, over the attachment for the plume, was the blue and white wool cockade; starting in 1809 it was made of painted lead. The caterpillar for the cavalry was taller and thicker and made of black wool. Pointed visor. The chinstraps were of black leather with brass reinforcement on the edges.

Dragoons, until 1811

White *Kollett* coats with short coattails and closed facings, which varied in shape. The collar was also white. The facings and cuffs were in the distinction color. White coattails with red edge trim and a retaining button in the middle.

Starting in 1804, white metal epaulets each with ten tin scales were worn on each shoulder. These scales were sewn onto red cloth. On the end was a ribbed crescent.

Regiment	Distinction	Buttons
1st	red	white metal
2nd	red	yellow metal

For parades, a red sash was worn around the waist.

Starting in March 1804, they wore close-fitting white pants with knee-high boots, with smooth tops, and strap-on spurs. In the field, long gray overall with wide red stripes and brass buttons down the seams. Loose-fitting gray overcoat. Black leather gloves with cuffs.

For camp duty, they wore the stable jacket, with a standing collar with a patch in the distinction color on each side. The jacket was closed in front with 16 leather buttons.

The forage cap was in the pattern of the chevaulegers; for the dragoons it was of gray cloth with white piping.

Dragoons

Top row: colonel 2nd Dragoon Regiment mounted with gala shabraque, dragoon 1st Dragoon Regiment in field attire
Bottom row: Rittmeister (captain) 1st Dragoon Regiment, trumpeter 2nd Dragoon Regiment, dragoon 1st Dragoon Regiment, dragoon 2nd Dragoon Regiment in camp attire

The lower part of the cap was white with a red border, and there was a red tassel on the peak.

The shabraque was of red cloth with a light blue and white diamond pattern border. The front portion was of white sheep's pelt with red wolf's teeth edging.

The saddlery was of black leather with white metal fittings.

Officers

Their uniform was like that of the troops with the following differences: silver sash worked through with blue silk. Cartridge box on a bandolier, both in silver.

Red rectangular cloth shabraque with pistol holster covers. The cloth was bordered by a double silver border. In the rear corner was the royal monogram with a crown above it.

Trumpeters

On the collar, facings and cuffs was a wide silver braid for the 1st Regiment; gilt for the 2nd Regiment. Trumpeter's wings on both shoulders were in red for their basic color and with a wide silver braid on both edges.

The 1st Regiment additionally had white swallow's nests with silver braid; on both sleeves were v-shaped chevrons in silver that were attached to one another.

In 1811 both dragoon regiments were converted to chevauleger regiments so that now this branch consisted of six regiments.

Chevaulegers

The caterpillar helmet (*Raupenhelm*) model introduced in 1800 corresponded to that for the dragoons. A white plume was inserted on the left side.

The forage cap was the same model as for the infantry but the bottom portion was dark green and had a tassel. The trim was in the regiment's distinction color, however, for units with a black distinction the edging was white. The peak was gray with green piping.

The cut of the *Kollet* coat was also identical with that for the dragoons and until 1809 was of light green or grass green cloth.

After the reorganization of the cavalry in November 1809, they changed the basic color to dark green or "steel" green and with short coattails also in the basic color. On the collar, cuffs and facings were in the distinction color; every two regiments had the same distinction color and were differentiated by their button color.

On the inside of the coattails was a 2cm (¾ in.) wide, L-shaped edging lace in the distinction color. On each coattail a standing lion and a crown were sewn on in white cloth as an emblem. In the middle of the coattail was vertical piping - for all regiments in red – running from the waist button to the end of the coattail.

Cuffs were like those for the dragoons with a patch with piping and four buttons in the distinction colors.

The neck sock was of black cloth with white stripes sewn on it.

Green vests with 8 small buttons were worn under the *Kollett* coat. Starting in December 1809, the vest was to be white.

Distinctions until 1809		
Regiment	Distinction Color	Button Color
Kronprinz	black piped white	white metal
2nd Koenig	black piped white	yellow metal
3rd Prinz Leiningen	green	white metal
4th Bubenhofen	green	yellow metal

Distinctions starting 29 April 1811			
Regiment	Distinction Color	Collar	Button Color
1st (without a title)	red	green	white metal
2nd Taxis	red	green	yellow metal
3rd Kronprinz	black with red piping	black	yellow metal
4th König	red	red	white metal
5th Prinz Leiningen	red	red	yellow metal
6th Bubenhofen	black with red piping		white metal

Starting in 1807, white metal scaled epaulets, with red cloth backing on both shoulders. The models varied among the regiments, so one-piece embossed epaulets multiple pieces in plates sewn next to each other.

Starting in 1804 they wore close-fitting white pants. In the field gray broad overalls with 16 leather buttons on the outside seams on each leg; additionally, stripes in the distinction color. In contemporary depictions the overalls are also shown with leather-inserts between the legs and going completely around the lower part of the leg, so that they give the impression of "false" boots. Starting in 1813, green overalls with colored stripes on the sides[66].

Knee-high leather boots for mounted duty. In the barracks and for dismounted duty they wore black leather shoes.

Starting in 1802, during bad weather, they wore a gray loden overcoat with sleeves and one row of buttons. On both sides of the standing collar were green laces with red piping and a retaining button in the regiment's button color.

---

66 *Officially introduced starting in 1818.*

Chevaulegers 1811
Trumpeter, 1st Regiment; Chevauleger 4th Regiment Koenig and 3rd Regiment Kronprinz
From Friedrich Münich, *Geschichte der Entwicklung der bay. Armee,* 1864

In addition, white or gray wool mittens were worn in the winter. For the 1809 campaign fingered gloves of mottled gray cloth were worn.

NCOs and troopers had gray cloth sashes that were only worn with the parade uniform. On the depictions, these were seldom shown.

The uniform for duty in camp or garrison, starting in 1809, was a sleeved, white cloth vest and the *"Holz-Lagermuetze"* forage cap.

The cartridge box of black leather and without an emblem, was worn on a white bandolier with brass buckles. Another bandolier with a hook was used to hold the carbine with the barrel pointing down and further secured to the shabraque.

The carbine was from Austria, but later produced in Amberg and had a caliber of 17.84 mm, weighed ca. 2.5 kilograms or 5.5 pounds and had a total length of 88 cm (34½").

The ramrod was attached to the bandolier with a white strap. The light curved saber had an iron basket hilt and scabbard. The blade was 84 cm (33") long. The sword knot was of white lacquered leather. The saber was worn over the *Kollet* coat on a white waist belt with a yellow buckle.

Shabraques were of scarlet red cloth coming to a point in the rear with a white and blue diamond-pattern edging. In the rear corner was the crowned cypher in white. The overcoat roll was round and had the diamond pattern circling it as a border. Black saddlery with white metal fittings.

NCOs

The helmet had a caterpillar made of hair like for the officers; the sword-strap was white with light blue stripes and a tassel. The *Wachtmeister* had a silver tassel with a red button on the saber strap. White cuffed gloves and hazelnut cane to indicate rank. The royal monogram in white was on the shabraque and in the front over the holsters. They did not carry carbines, but only pistols.

Officers

The *Kaskett*/helmet was like that for the infantry but taller and could reach a height of 44 cm (17"). The brass parts were gilded. The bearskin caterpillar was taller and protruding. A white feather plume was attached on the side.

The coats were of a darker tone and often appeared almost black. The coattail emblems were silver-plated. In the field were buttoned over and mostly turned so that the distinction color was only visible in the upper portion.

White narrow pants were worn for parades; and starting in April 1804, long gray overalls with stripes on the side in the distinction color were worn for protection in the field.

Starting the end of 1808, for informal duty and for parades they wore close-fitting pants; in the field they wore long green trousers with red stripes on the sides. Often unapproved additional metal buttons were added to the stripes on the sides.

Starting in 1802, they had gray overcoats with a small standing collar and large cape. On the standing collar was a gold or silver braid in the appropriate button color. White or often also black cuffed gloves.

Until April 1812, a sash, then it was abolished. For this purpose, the cartridge box bandolier of red saffron leather decorated with silver and light blue striped borders. The cartridge was red box with a silver lid on which an embossed King's monogram was visible. At chest level there was a lion's head silver plate from which were hung two clearing needles (for the pistols).

These were stuck into a silver plate somewhat lower on the bandolier. The royal cypher was on that plate.

Red leather waist belt had silver and blue streaked edges. Sword knot was silver also with four light blue silk threads interwoven.

The shabraque was red with silver trim and in the front and rear corners were the gilded embroidered royal monogram surrounded by a laurel wreath. Senior/staff officers' shabraques had a double braid edging with and additional fringe rim in the regiment's button color.

The temporary shabraques were also red, however with narrower borders. For gala events, on the other hand, they had a double surrounding border.

Trumpeters

A red plume on the *Kaskett* helmet.

In general, the musicians wore the same uniform and colors as the troops, however, starting in 1804, they had braid edging on the collar, cuffs and facings in gold or silver according to the button color.

On their backs, they had trim of cloth stripes, the so-called "trumpeter's wings" as false sleeves in the distinction color.

White cuffed gloves.

The gala uniform had variations depending on the Regiment commander's wishes, mostly, however, the coat was in the distinction color and facings green.

Signal trumpets had a 1 cm (7/16") wide blue and white cord with two tassels on the end. They were positioned over the trumpeter's left shoulder or on his back.

Regimental or Staff Trumpeter: a double braid on the cuffs and collar.

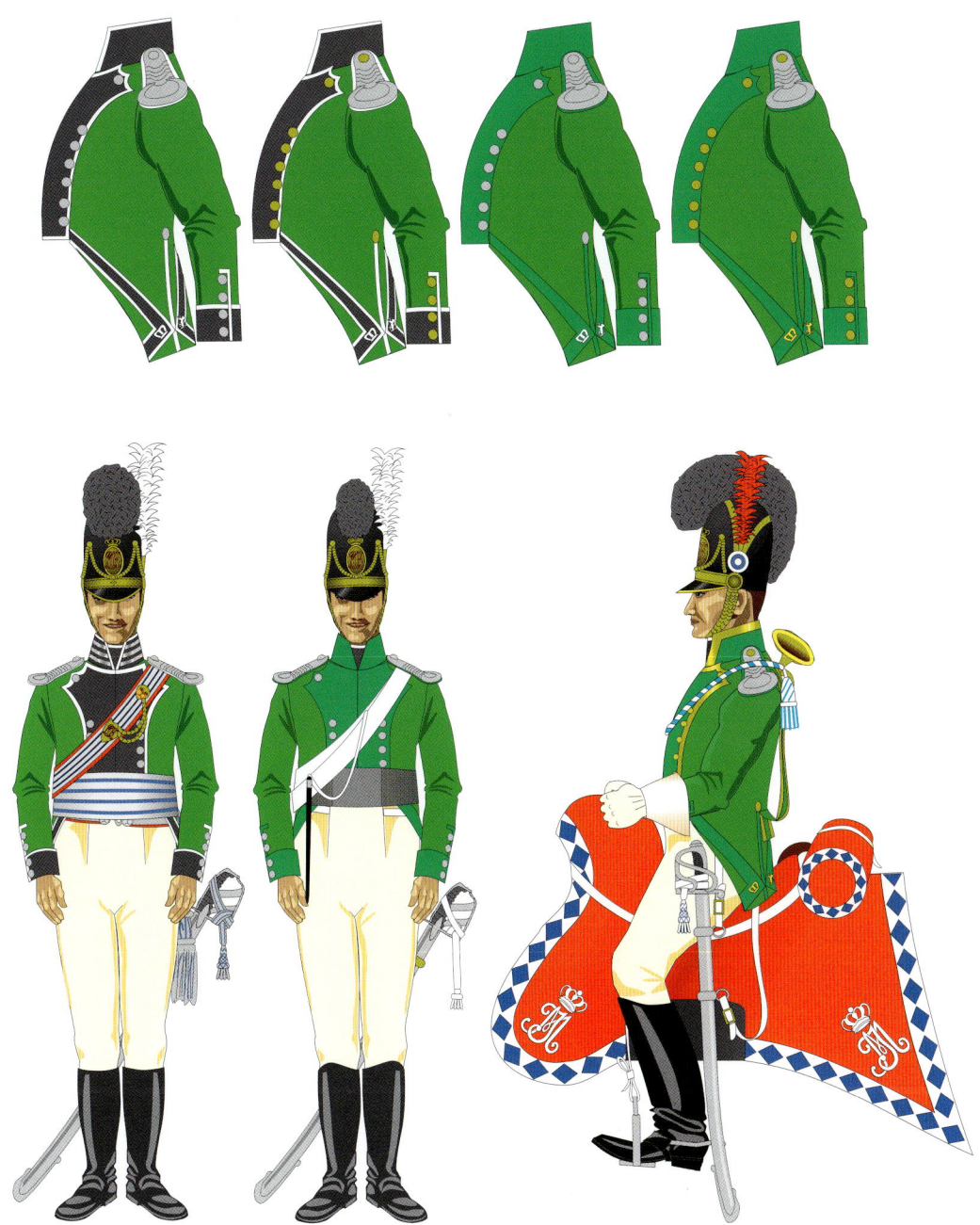

Chevaulegers 1806 – 1809

Top row: Coat patterns 1st through 4th Chevauleger Regiments
Bottom row: Rittmeister (captain) 1st Regiment, chevauleger 3rd Regiment, trumpeter 4th Regiment

Colonel of Chevaulegers Regiment No. 2 and captain of the light artillery before 1812
Engraving by Venturini, from the collection of M. Gärtner

Trumpeter National-Chevauleger Regiment 1813
Watercolor by Eduard Kohler, Anne S.K. Brown Military Collection, Brown University Library, Providence, USA

According to various sources and depictions the individual regiments' variations to or unofficial uniforms looked as follows:

1st Regt.
Red *Kollet* with green distinctions and silver lacing. Green trumpeter's wings were edged in silver[67].

2nd Regt.
Red *Kollet* with white distinctions and golden braid edging. Trumpeter's wings were whited edged in gold.[68]

2nd Regt. - Variation
Light blue *Kollet* with black distinctions, silver trim. Trumpeter's wings black, edged in silver. Around 1807 they had a black bicorn with silver laces and a short black and white short. Starting in 1811, they had a *Kaskett* with a red hanging plume[69].

3rd Regt.
On the facings additional yellow laces and black swallows nests with yellow edging[70].

4th Regt.
Starting in 1809 for parades and gala events, red *Kollets* with green distinctions; the *Kaskett* had a red hanging plume[71].

5th Regiment
Additional yellow laces on the facings, yellow under the scaled epaulets, swallows nests and chevrons on both sleeves in the distinction color[72].
Variants: without laces or chevrons[73]

---

67 According to illustrations by Herbert Knötel and depictions by Henri Boisselier.
68 According to the Marckolsheim manuscript, probably the reversed dragoon coat.
69 According to drawings by Peter Wacker and depictions by Henri Boisselier.
70 According to J. Arnold, private series of plates from around 1920.
71 According to Cantler, plate 311.
72 According to Tanconville.
73 According to Albrecht Adam.

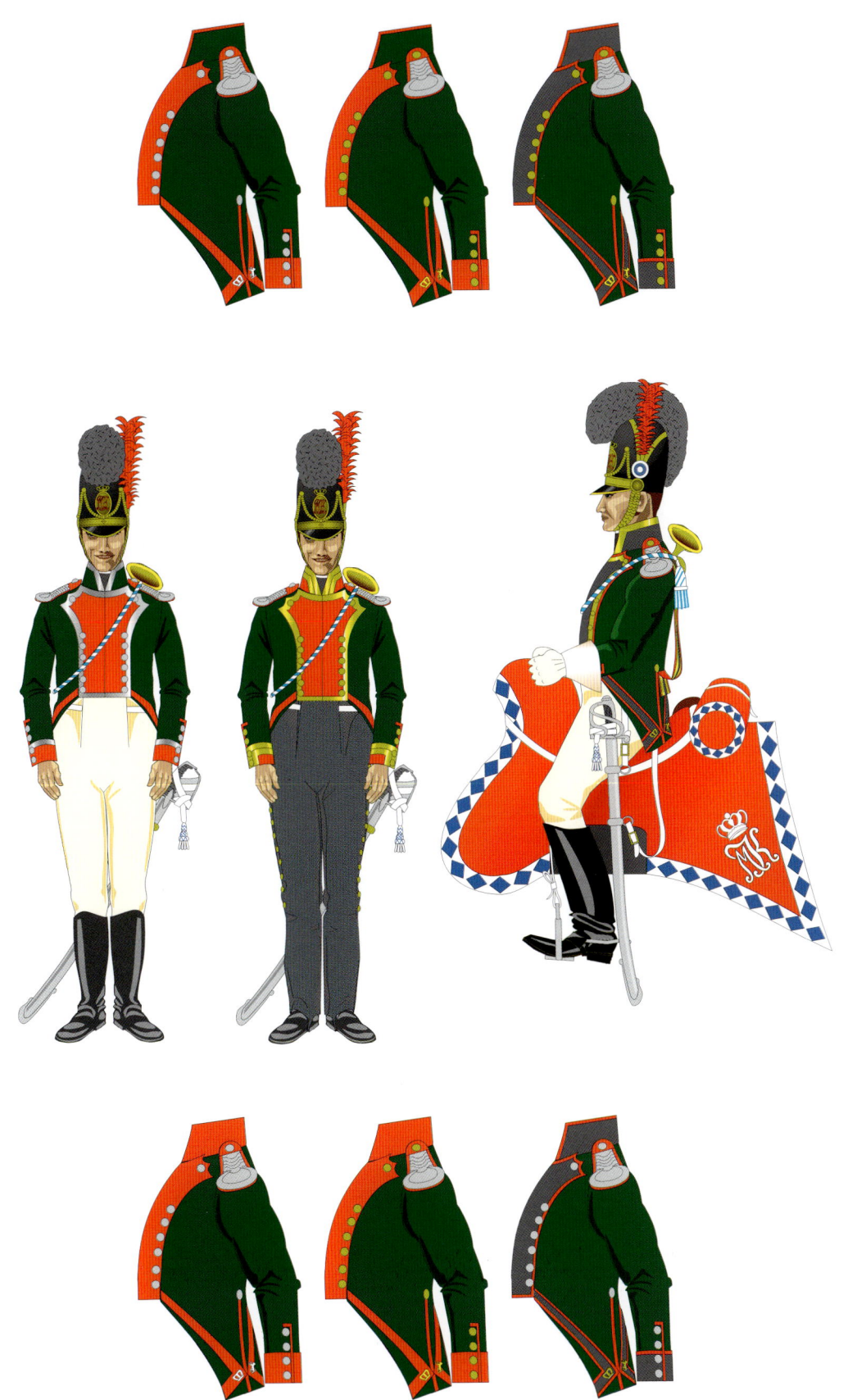

Chevaulegers 1811 Coat patterns, trumpeters

Top row: coat patterns 1st Regiment, 2nd Regiment Taxis, 3rd Regiment Kronprinz
Middle row: trumpeter 1st Regiment, staff trumpeter 5th Regiment Leiningen in field dress, trumpeter 3rd Regiment Kronprinz mounted
Bottom row: Coat patterns 4th Regiment Koenig, 5th Regiment Leiningen, 6th Regiment Bubenhofen

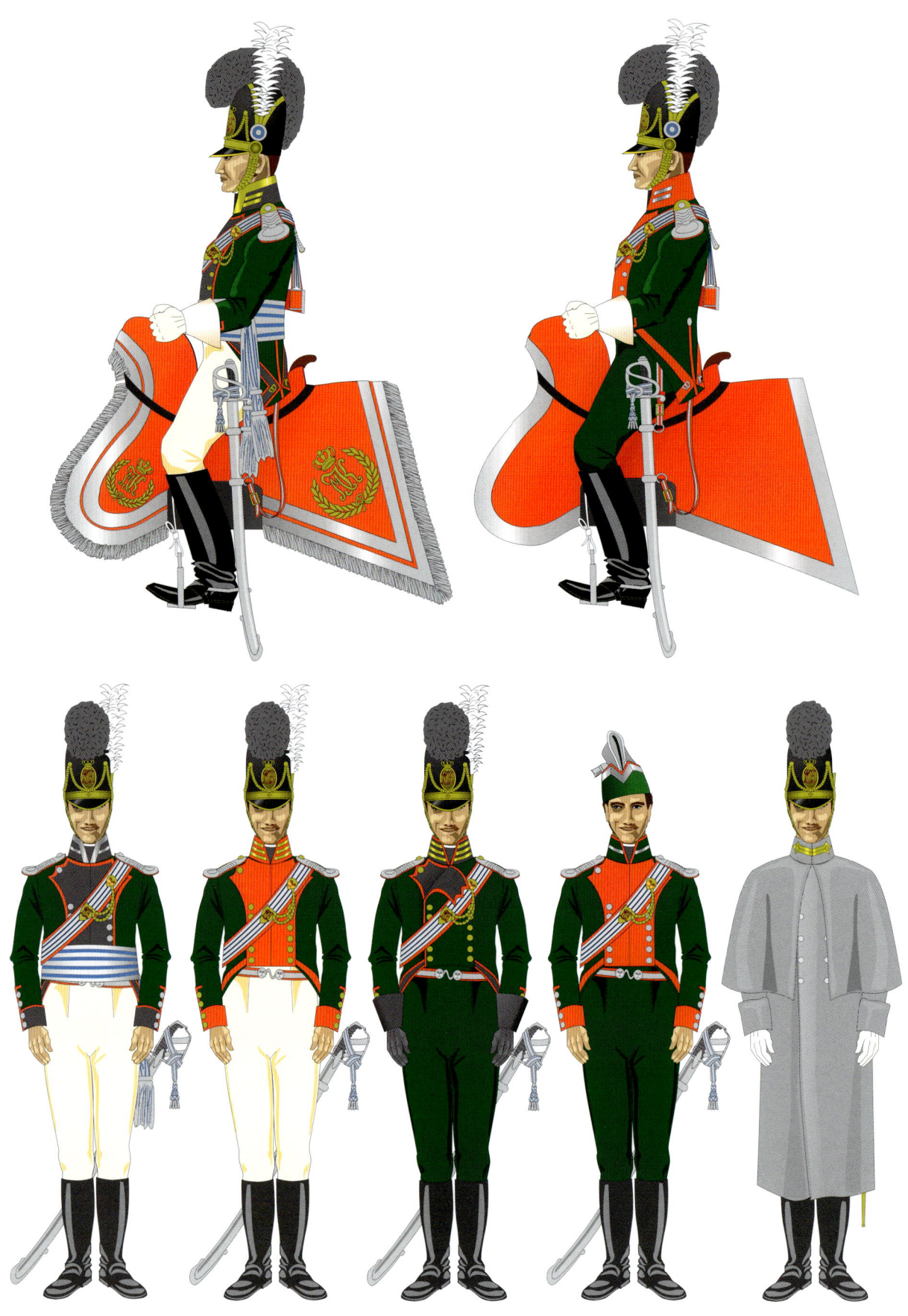

Chevaulegers 1811 - Officers

Top row: Lieutenant colonel 3rd Regiment Kronprinz with gala shabraque, premier/senior lieutenant 4th Regiment König service uniform
Bottom row: Major 6th Regiment Bubenhofen until 1812, *Rittmeister* (captain) 5th Regiment Leiningen starting in 1812, *Rittmeister* 3rd Regiment Kronprinz field dress, second lieutenant 1st Regiment with forage cap, officer in an overcoat

Chevaulegers 1811 – Enlisted Troops

Top row: NCO 6th Regiment Bubenhofen, chevauleger 2nd Regiment Taxis mounted
Bottom row: chevauleger 5th Regiment Leiningen, chevauleger 3rd Regiment Kronprinz field dress, chevauleger 6th Regiment Bubenhofen, chevauleger in camp uniform, chevauleger in an overcoat

Trumpeters of the 1st and 2nd regiment Chevaulegers 1812-1813 by Henri Boisselier,
Anne S.K. Brown Military Collection, Providence, USA

Trumpeter of the 3rd regiment Chevaulgers 1812-1813 by Henri Boisselier,
Anne S.K. Brown Military Collection, Providence, USA

Regiments' Horse Colors

For officers and enlisted troops, it appears that specific colors were not prescribed; for the trumpeters and NCOs the following colors were named[74]:

Regt	Trumpeter	Corporal	Wachtmeister
1st	chestnut without markings	white	light brown
2nd	dun	black	white
3rd	white	light brown	dark chestnut
4th	chestnut with blazes	white	light brown
5th	light gray	dark brown	chestnut
6th	peibald	light brown	black

The National Chevauleger Regiment – starting 1813 the 7th Regiment Prinz Karl

The shako, with a cockade, had white cording and hanging feather plume. The skirmishers (*Plänkler*) stuck on a green feather plume to distinguish themselves. On the shako's front was an oval plate and band, both of brass. The green coat was single-breasted with a red collar, cuffs and piping. Buttons were white metal. The close-fitting green pants were worn inside knee-length smooth boots. In the field they wore overalls with stripes on the sides and leather inserts reaching to the calves.

NCOs had a white band on the shako rim.

The red cloth shabraque come to a point in the back, with a white border without the diamond pattern.

Officers

A shako, like for the troops, with a white plume and cording, and the shako band in silver. Cartridge box and bandolier were like for the chevaulegers.

The shabraque had silver trim; for the senior/staff officers it had an additional fringe.

Trumpeters

On the upper shako rim was a wide white braid. A hanging red feather plume was attached in the front.

The red coat had green distinctions and silver trumpeter's wings. Green pants with red stripes on the sides. Long trousers in the same color were worn in the field.

---

74 According to G.W. Fricke/W. Friedrich, Bayern 1812/13

Military Officials 1804-1815
Furier and Provost, **Auditor, Staff Doctor and War Commisar** (*Kriegskommisar*)
From Friedrich Münich, *Geschichte der Entwicklung der bay. Armee,* **1864**

TECHNICAL TROOPS (ROYAL ARTILLERY CORPS)

Foot Artillery (*Artillerie zu Fuß*)

Starting in 1801, the headgear was the same *Kaskett* model, the *Raupenhelm*, as the infantry. The band of brass on the front, that ran across above the visor had the inscription: ARTILLERIE REGIMENT. A cockade was located on the left chin-scale chain and above it was the red wool plume - the *"Huppette"*.

The coat was dark blue with black distinctions piped in red.

The coattails were red. Starting in 1807, the shoulder pieces here, even though they were dismounted troops, also consisted of brass scales on a red cloth backing. Yellow metal buttons. Dark blue tight pants, worn with black cloth gaiters, which were closed on the sides with yellow buttons. In the field, long white trousers were also worn.

The white leather bandoliers were worn crossed over the shoulders. Starting in 1808, a pack was worn on the back like for the die infantry. The gray overcoat collar was trimmed with a red patch. In the field, overcoat was carried rolled up over the shoulder.

Until 1808, for casual duty (in garrison), white and bleu striped loose-fitting pants were used, afterwards, also white trousers were worn.

Along with that a single-breasted, sleeved vest (*"Kamisol"*) and a blue forage cap with red piping and a red tassel were worn.

For armament until 1807, they carried a short grenadier saber with a brass grip on a waist belt. Starting in 1803, additionally they carried a pistol in a holster suspended from a bandolier worn over the shoulder. In 1807 a fascine knife (*"Faschinenmesser"*) was introduced that had a straight blade and a brass handle in the shape of a stylized lion's head.

Starting in January 1812, 50 men in each company were equipped with infantry muskets and cartridge boxes. In response, their pistols were turned in.

NCOs

They wore the same uniform as the troops with the following differences – the NCOs' *Kaskett* had a taller bearskin caterpillar crest; and short riding boots instead of gaiters (starting April 1806). The NCO cane was hung from the second button on the left. Additionally, the basket hilt saber had a silver tassel like for the infantry.

Officers

Starting in 1809 they also the *Kaskett* that corresponded to the infantry model and had a taller crest made of bearskin.

Starting in February 1806, a red feather plume was attached to the *Kaskett's* left side. The coat had long Coattails like for the infantry. The coattails were decorated with gilded grenade emblems.

Black stovepipe boots.

In the field and for casual duty a single-breasted frock coat was worn.

Until 1812 along with the rank insignia on the collar, they wore the silver sash with blue interweaving, and then they wore the silver gorget with the coat of arms like for the other branches' officers.

The officer's overcoat was gray and had a broad cape. There was a golden patch on the collar. Mounted officers wore black leather cuffed gloves.

Until 1808 the cavalry saber was the armament. Afterward, the company-grade officers had unapproved swords with a silver and blue sword knot.

The officers were mounted and used blue cloth shabraques with a gilded border and red piping. The pistol holsters were covered with a hide.

For gala dress they had a red shabraque and pistol holster covers with gilded braid edging. In the rear corners they additionally had the royal cypher.

Drummer

Uniform like for the troops and starting in 1805 with red swallows nests surrounded with yellow edge trim on both shoulders. Starting in April 1811, in the center of the swallows nest was the royal monogram inside a white cloak. Later, scaled epaulets were added on both shoulders. Both sleeves were conspicuously decorated with 5 wide yellow chevrons that were connected to the lace on the sleeves' seams. Furthermore there was a yellow edging lace on the facings, on the collar and cuffs.

The model of drum corresponded to that of the infantry. A short white leather half-apron was worn tied under the knee.

The regimental drummer had double braiding on the collar and cuffs.

Regimental Music starting in 1812

As the gala uniform, the musicians wore a single-breasted blue frock coat that was conspicuously decorated on the chest with elaborate horizontal lacing. The collar and cuffs had golden edging. White pants and boots. As Headgear a bicorn hat with golden trim and a red feather plume.

For the undress uniform a simple bicorn hat. Frock coat without trim and long blue cloth trousers.

For armament they had a short saber.

The drum major had a double edging braid on the collar cuffs.

A wide black bandolier, bordered with gold and red was worn over the shoulder. At chest level it had two small brass drum loops and two small drumsticks.

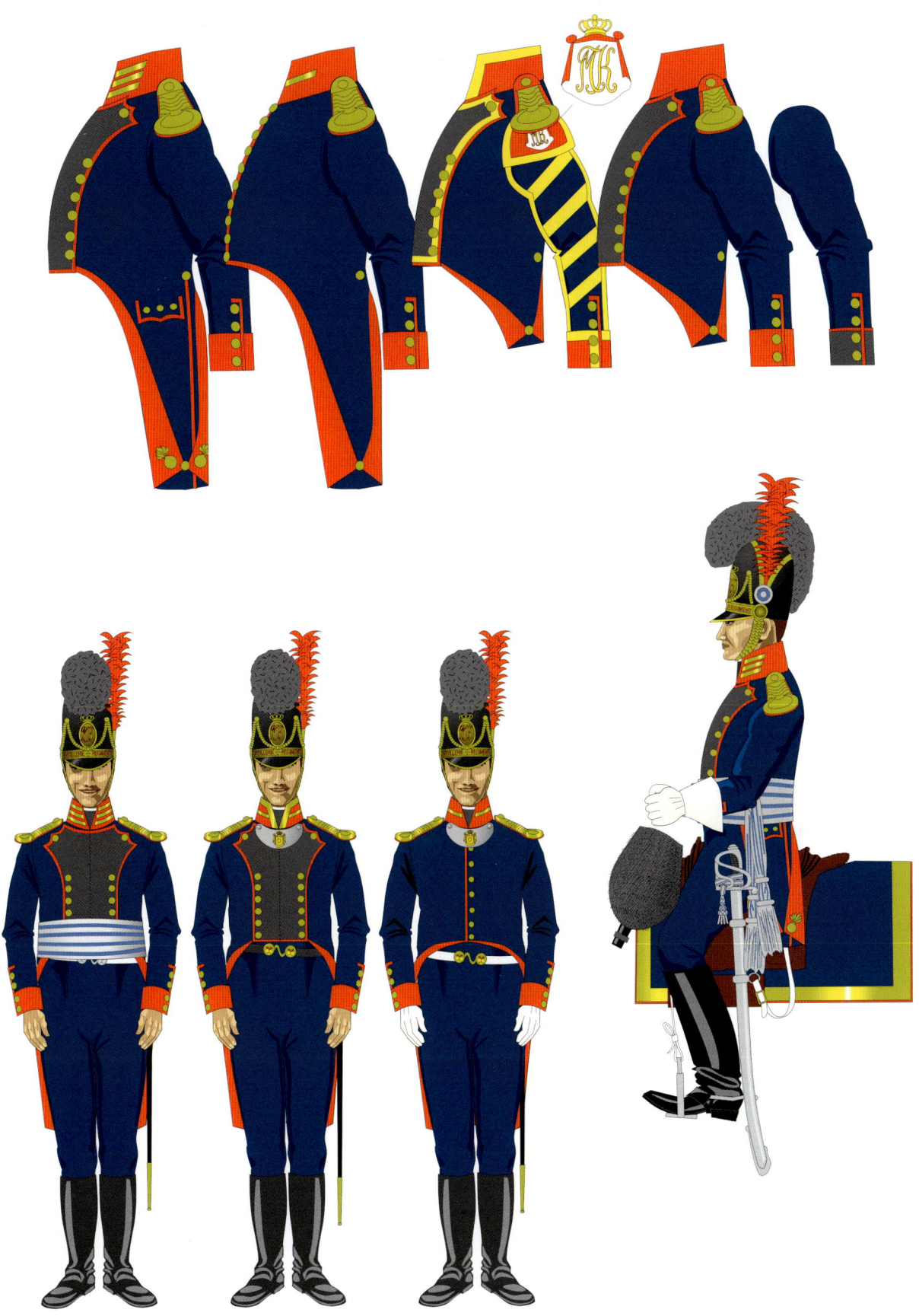

Foot Artillery - Officers' Coat Patterns

Top row: coat patterns: officer's coat, officer's frock coat, drummer, artilleryman, *Ouvrier's* sleeve detail
Bottom row: captain until 1812, major starting in 1812, premier lieutenant in frock coat starting in 1812, mounted captain until 1812

The drumsticks had silver-plated metal butts and tips as well as silver cording around the shaft.

Ouvriers (Artisans - Handwerker Workers)

Starting in September 1811, the artisans received the same uniform as the artillery with the difference that the sleeve distinctions were black instead of red.

The *Werkstattmeister*, in the rank of a senior NCO (*Feldwebel*) and the *Zeugwart*, in the rank of a second lieutenant had "new model" bicorns," as well as epaulets on both shoulders, and boots and NCO's insignia.

The *Oberfeuerwerker* or *Wachtmeister* wore officers' coats and carried NCO's basket-hilt sabers.

Arsenal Administration (Main Directorate) Zeughaus-Verwaltung (Hauptdirektion)

Together with the *Ouvrier* Company. Uniform like the artillery, however long coats, and instead of the *Kaskett* they had the bicorn hat.

Light Artillery/Batteries

The headgear was the same *Kaskett* model with side braces like for the Chevaulegers, and with a red plume attached on the left side. The inscription ARTILLERIE-REGIMENT was embossed into the brass band.

The dark blue coat had short coattails and the cut like the chevaulegers. The distinction color and piping like for the foot artillery. The coattails had yellow grenades as emblems. They also had scaled epaulets.

Dark blue close-fitting pants were worn with gaiters. In the field they wore long dark blue, with leather reinforcements on the insides, riding pants.

Weapons and equipment were like for the foot batteries.

The NCOs were mounted and instead of gaiters they wore boots that reached to just under the knees.

For armament they had the cavalry saber and their pistols were carried on the horse equipment, and the cartridge box on a white bandolier over the left shoulder. White cuffed gloves were worn for mounted duty.

The shabraque had a sheep's pelt with red wolf's teeth in the front, and sewn to the back was a short rectangular dark blue cloth portion with red edging lace, all worn over a Hungarian-English saddle.

Trumpeters[75]

Uniform like for the troops, however it had yellow lace edging on the facings, collar and cuffs. For gala wear, trumpeter's wings were attached to the back and they were made of blue cloth with broad gold trim and edged in red. Starting in 1812, one also saw a variant with red fringes on the epaulets and contrary to regulations a hanging feather plume on the Kaskett helmet.

Because these cadres were mounted, they had boots as footgear that reached to just below the knee. The shabraque were like those for the NCOs.

The trumpet was made of brass and slung on a silver cord interwoven with light blue and two tassels. As armament they carried the cavalry saber.

Officers

The uniform was cut like that for cavalry officers; the coat however had long coattails. Until 1812, they wore a sash, and then it was abolished. In its place they wore a broad cavalry bandolier of black leather with gold trim on both sides. At chest level was a small chain with clearing needles on a plate in the shape of a lion's head. The cartridge box was also black with a metal cover. On the lid was the gilded royal monogram with a crown. The saber was in an iron scabbard on a black leather belt. For mounted duty they wore black, cuffed gloves.

Undress Uniform

Starting in 1810, the shabraque was of rectangular dark blue cloth with a gold border and red piping. On both sides were pistol holsters with bearskin covers.

For gala attire, senior/staff officers had red cloth shabraques and pistol holster covers with triple border lace and red piping, and the royal cypher in the corners.

Army Transport System (*Armee-Fuhrwesen*)

Starting in 1806, the "Train" was organized as a military entity and adopted the uniform of the cavalry or the light artillery with the following differences:

The *Kaskett* helmet had no plume or brass front band or inscription.

The single-breasted coat in the chevauleger's pattern was of light iron gray. The collar and the cuffs were light blue, and the coattails light gray piped with a light blue border. In the front, the seam was closed with 9 pewter buttons and piped with light blue. White metal, scaled epaulets had light blue cloth backings.

On the left arm, the troops wore a blue cloth band that had a metal shield in the middle. On the shield the monogram "MJK" was embossed.

Starting in 1806, they wore long gray pants with light blue stripes on the sides, and on the insides were reinforced with was brown leather. As a variation, the pants could also be stuck into the knee-length boots.

For undress duty they wore the forage cap with light blue piping and a tassel.

Their gray overcoats had no trim.

Until 1808, they had no weapons, and after that a short saber[76] carried on a black leather shoulder bandolier. They had black leather cuffed gloves.

---

[75] Since April 1811.

[76] Sabers were at first obtained at their own expense by the troops who not were viewed "as soldiers" until 1806.

Foot Artillery – Enlisted Troops

Top row: drummer, NCO, artilleryman, artilleryman with musket starting 1811, artilleryman in working attire
Bottom row: artilleryman with work pants 1807, artilleryman with work pants starting in 1808 (front and back), Workshop Master (*Werkstattmeister*) of the Artisan (*Ouvrier*) company, captain of the Engineer Corps (*Ingenieur-Korps*)

NCOs wore the cavalry saber on a white waist belt, and additionally had a shoulder bandolier with a cartridge box

Trumpeters

Had white border trim on the collar and cuffs. On the back of the coat they had light blue trumpeter's wings, with wide silver borders on the sides.

Like for the artillery, the NCOs and trumpeters were mounted and used, like the earlier dragoons, a white sheep's pelt shabraque with red wolf's teeth and a red cloth blanket sewn on the rear with a white and blue diamond pattern border. In the corners, the royal monogram was in white.

Officers

The coat was cut like that of the infantry with light blue facings and long coattails. Coattail turn-backs and vertical pocket piping were light blue. They wore gray close-fitting pants without stripes on the sides and boots.

Epaulets and buttons were silver-plated.

The officers also had a single-breasted frock coat as a second outfit.

From 1807 until 1812 the sash was worn, then in 1812 abolished again. Black cuffed gloves.

The light cavalry saber was carried on a waist belt. The silver-plated belt buckle showed the "MJK" royal cypher under a crown.

Starting in 1812, the cartridge box was on a black bandolier like for the artillery. Both were decorated with silver-plated plates.

Company-grade officers had black sheep's pelt shabraques with red wolf's teeth, and the attached cloth blanket was gray with silver edging.

The battalion commandant's parade shabraque had a double border lace with a fringe on the outside.

Engineers (*Ingenieure*)

This was a small organization ("*kleines Korps*") and consisted only of officers of varying ranks; it was subordinate to the General Staff. Starting in 1805, they wore the caterpillar helmet (*Raupenhelm*), however without the feather plume. The uniform corresponded to the one of the artillery officers with black facings and red collar. To distinguish the engineers from artillery they had silver buttons and rank insignia.Until 1812, the sash was worn, and afterward the gorget was worn. Starting in 1803, gray overcoats were worn in inclement weather.

Starting in 1812, instead of the white belt, ones of polished black leather with white fittings and a lion's head buckle were worn. A cavalry saber served as armament.

Painting of Artillery Pieces

The cannon barrels were of shiny bronze and were mounted on gray gun carriages with black polished metal fittings.

Military Administration

All officials (*Kriegskommissar*/war commissioner, administration, and justice like auditors, medical personnel) and various ranks with functions in the Administration generally had the same uniform, whereby until 1809 -12 the coats produced under the August 1799 regulations were often used. Officially, for the first time in 1822, a regulation on the uniforms for this branch was issued again. So it is not surprising that varying models and styles of uniforms were used at the same time. Starting in 1812, one paid more attention to fashions trends and the military officials and the medical personnel wore the following attire:

The bicorn hat had a gilded hat clasp and cockade. The single-breasted dark blue coat was closed in front with 9 buttons and had long coattails. The collar and cuffs were red. The coattails were also red with the front seam in the same color. Starting in 1804, a white undervest was worn. Close-fitting white pants were worn with knee-high boots.

For armament, they had a sword with a silver sword knot, carried on a white leather waist belt. White gloves.

The rank was displayed on the collar and cuffs by a silver braid or embroidery.

Unterbeamter (Junior Official, i.e., *Employee* and *Aktuare* [dispatch writer]): no embroidery: no embroidery.

Beamter (secretary or *Sekretaer*): with golden lace on the collar and cuffs.

Kriegskommissar: double lace. For casual duty dark blue Provost (trousers.

Provost (*Profos*): White hat clasp on the bicorn. The coat was light brown with a red collar and cuffs as well as piping.

Auditor (*Auditeur*): The coat had blue cuffs, and silver buttons and braid on the collar and cuffs.

Starting in 1804, the attire for the doctors was standardized and was aligned with the uniforms of the senior officials with the following differences.

Doctor/Staff Doctor (*Arzt/Stabsarzt*) for the General Staff: The hat clasp, edging and buttons were silver-plated.

Battalion surgeon: Had no sword knot, and in the field wore blue or white cloth trousers.

Regimental surgeon 1812: Had three silver horizontal laces on the collar.

Military pharmacist (*Militärapotheker*): red standing collar without braid.

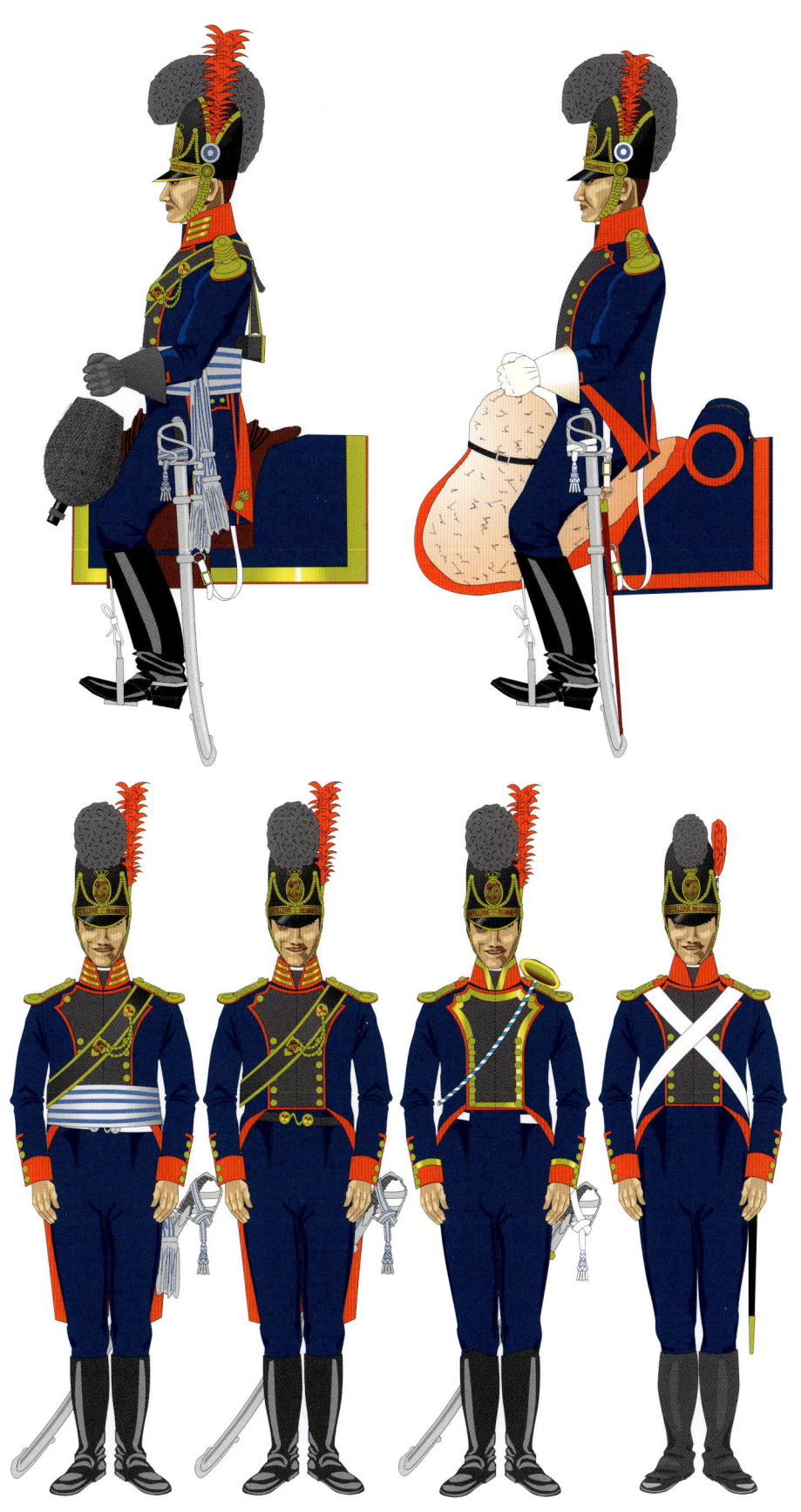

Light Artillery

Top row: mounted captain until 1812, mounted NCO
Bottom row: captain until 1812, captain starting in 1812, trumpeter, artilleryman

Gendarmerie 1812
Engraving "Die bayerische Armee 1813-1826", by J. Volz
Collection M. Gärtner

Train

Top row: mounted lieutenant colonel starting in 1812, mounted NCO
Bottom row: captain until 1812, premier lieutenant starting in 1812 in the frock coat, trumpeter, driver

Veterinarians

Senior Horse Doctor (*Ober-Pferdearzt*): Red Collar and dark blue cuffs. The collar and cuffs had two horizontal laces each; also the coat pockets had silver vertical laces. Cavalry boots without cuffs. Saber as for Chevaulegers with sword knot.

Regimental Horse Doctor (*Regiments-Pferdearzt*): The collar, coattails and front seam were red; the cuffs were blue. The collar and cuffs had a silver braid. The dark blue under-vest had silver lace decoration; starting in 1804 the vest was white.

Commandants (Kommandantschaften)

Bicorn hat with a broad wavy silver border. The coat had long coattails of cornflower blue cloth and a red collar. The distinctions were black velvet facings and cuffs with white metal buttons. The distinctions were piped with white. Close-fitting pants were worn with knee length boots.

The armament was a sword with a sword knot.

Officer of the Suite (Offizier a la Suite)

The bicorn hat had no decoration, but a white agrafe with a cockade on the front. The cornflower blue coat had long red coattails while the collar, facings and cuffs were in the black velvet distinction material. The buttons were white metal. White pants were worn with knee length boots.

The officers had the infantry's yellow under-vests and as a sward as a weapon.

The cavalry officers had white under-vests and the cavalry saber as armament.

Retired and Resigned (Quittierte) Officers

The bicorn hat had only the agrafe and cockade. The single-breasted dark blue coat had a light blue collar and cuffs, while the piping and buttons were white. On the collar was a lace or laces depending on rank. Long white pants.

Resigned officers (*Quittierte*) wore a cornflower blue coat with black collar, lapels and cuffs as the distinction. They also had the rank laces on the collar.

Cavalry had a white under-vest and a saber; the infantry had a yellow under-vest with a sword.

Nationalgarde 2. Klasse - Mobile Legions

In July 1809, the Mobile Legions were raised to support the standing army. In any case the actual formed battalions existed only very brief. In November they were disbanded again. The new creation of these formations only took place again in 1813.

The shako was made of felt with a brass band across the lower front rim. On the upper shako rim was a white band. The sharpshooter section stuck a short green plume on the shako. The battalions were differentiated by the colored rosettes on the side of the headgear – 1st Battalion red, 2nd white, 3rd blue, 4th yellow, and 5th red with black. On the front was a cockade with a white agrafe.

The uniform was supposed to consist of a dark blue coat with light blue distinctions, white metal buttons, white linen pants and white gaiters. Most of the troops could only be equipped with the gray overcoat with a light blue collar. City or traditional country attire was worn under the overcoat. They were equipped with muskets and cartridge boxes on white leather bandoliers, however, no sabers. The sharpshooters had *Stutzen* rifles or flintlocks with rifled barrels. The bread bag was of white denim.

NCOs

On the upper shako rim was a white camelhair braid, for the *Feldwebel* it was doubled. Basket-hilted saber and tassel like for the infantry.

Officers

The upper shako rim was in silver.

The single-breasted coat had light blue distinctions and had epaulets as rank insignia, but no sash.

Dark blue close-fitting pants or broad white trousers. The sword with a silver sword knot was carried on a waist belt.

After the Bavarian Army's heavy losses in 1812, they began to organize the reserves again. In February 1813, issuing of uniforms began, but they differed from the earlier ones.

The shako received an oval plate like the Line, but instead of the company rosettes, pompoms in the respective colors were added. The officers had silver pompoms.

The coat and pants were now light blue[77]. The collar, cuffs, piping and coattails were in the red distinction color.

The overcoat received a red standing collar. The officers had no epaulets, so instead they used the rank insignia of the Line; the gorget served as an additional rank distinction.

Drummers had red swallows nests with white trim and three white chevrons on each sleeve that touched the lace along the sleeves' seams.

Military Police (*Gendarmerie*)

This new force was established by the decree of 8 November 1812 to guarantee a permanent police force in the kingdom.

The shako had a red feather plume for the mounted Gendarmes, while the foot detachment had a red pompom. The coat was green and in the same cut as the

---

[77] *According to Peter Hess, with red stripes down the sides (1814).*

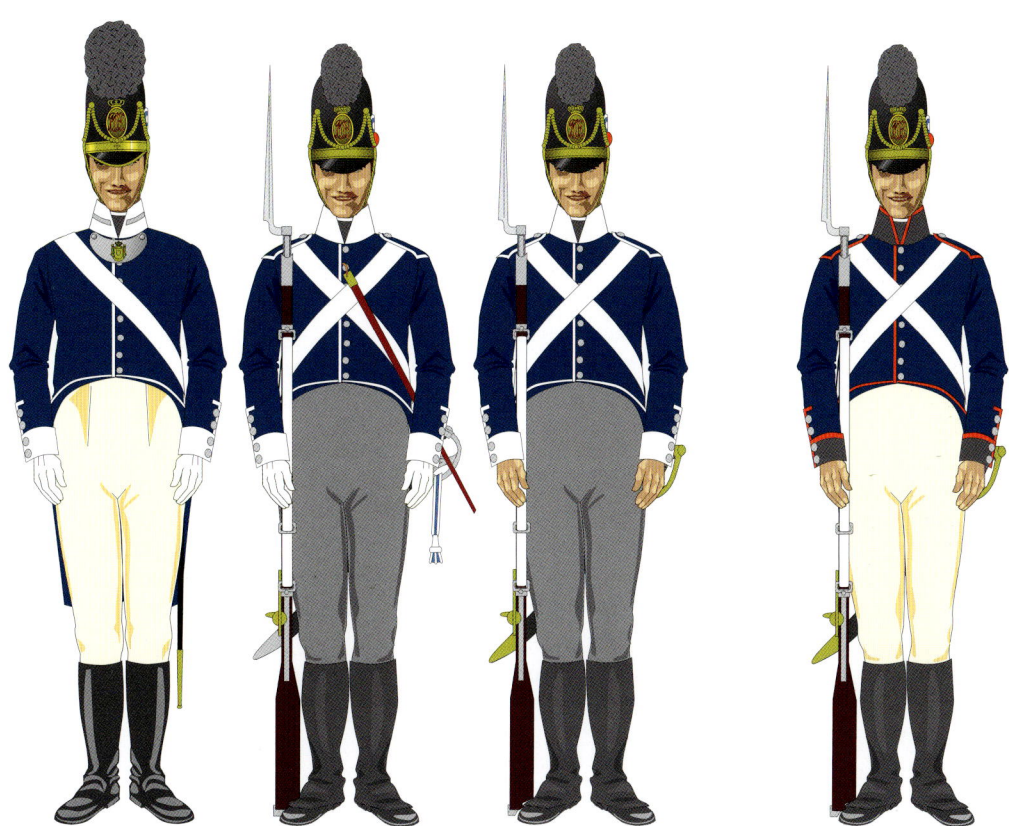

Hartschiere, Garrison Companies, Cadets

Top row: Hartschiere: adjutant and *Hartschier* in service uniform, *Hartschier* in Gala
Bottom row: garrison companies: officer, NCO, soldier, cadet

Mobile Legions and National Regiments

Top row: Mobile Legions: *Premier-Lieutenant*, drummer, legionnaire in work pants, sharpshooter (*Schütze*)
Bottom row: National Chevauleger Regiment: captain (*Rittmeister*), chevauleger in field uniform, mounted chevauleger

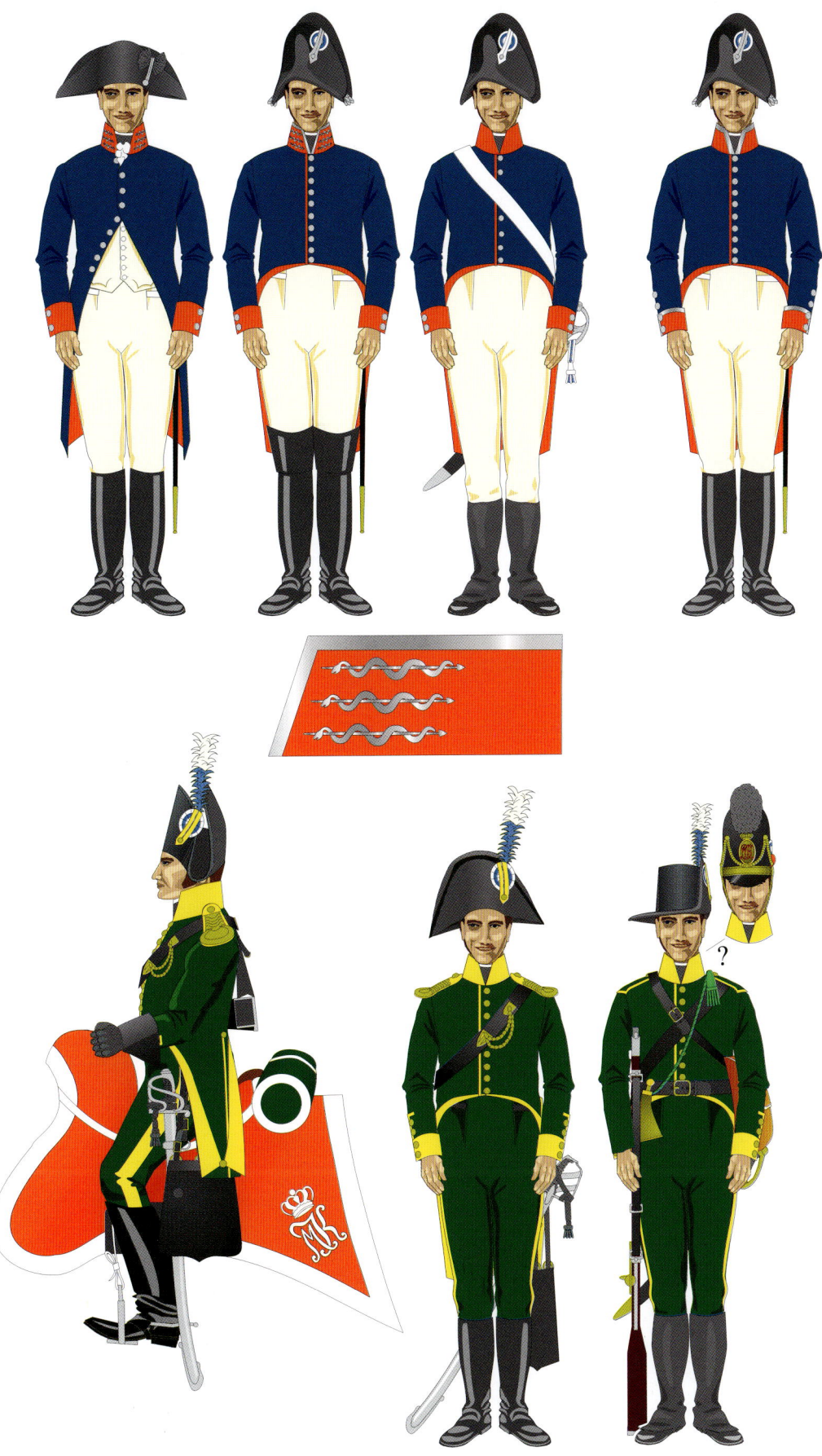

Doctors, Officials, Military Police (*Feldjäger*)

Top row: Regimental doctor 1806, Regimental doctor 1812, surgeon's assistant 1812, military official regimental doctor's collar embroidery
Bottom row: Mounted Field Jaeger (*berittener Feldjäger*) with saddlery, *berittener Feldjäger*, Foot Field Jaeger (*Feldjäger zu Fuß*)

chevaulegers, however with long coattails, had yellow metal buttons, and a red aiguillette on the shoulder.

The mounted detachment had shabraques like the chevaulegers, however the basic color was green. For armament they had a saber, carbine and two pistols carried in the pistol holster with covers.

The foot detachment had an infantry saber and a musket with a bayonet instead of the carbine.

Field Postal Service (*Feldpost*)

Starting in 1805, postal system was the responsibility of the Electoral Prince, later the King and the postmen received a light blue uniform with black cuffs. Their bicorn hat a wide white braid edging and a white cockade and agrafe, and an erect white and blue plume. The *Kollet* coat had short coattails and the facings were open in the front. The cuffs had a white braid. On the left upper arm was a black band with white edging and a white metal shield with the coat of arms. The red vest also had a white edging. Close-fitting white pants were worn with high riding boots. The postal horn was made of brass and hung on a white and blue cord with similarly colored tassels.

Weapons[78]

Until 1800 the firearms were of inferior quality and varied. Furthermore, due to the seizure of the contents of the arsenal by French forces, the situation for the Bavarian Army was more than questionable. By General von Manson's[79] establishing the firearms factory in Amberg in 1801, an independent model could be produced, however, not in the quantities needed. An additional factory in Fortschau could make a tiny number – 300 muskets per year, which only slightly improved the situation. Under Manon's leadership a new model musket was developed that was equipped with the old caliber and a new cylindrical ramrod. The model had a length of 146 cm (4'9"); in addition it had a 47 cm (18½") long four-edged bayonet. Starting in 1804, it was produced in Amberg. The first products went to the 1st Line Infantry Regiment and the Leib Regiment, while a small number went into the arsenal as a reserve. However, until 1805-06 only 2,131 of the 6,000 needed weapons could be produced.

Along with the infantry musket Models 1801 and 1804 it produced the M 1804 cavalry pistol and the M 1807 *"Jägerstutzen"* (hunting rifle). Additionally Austrian models were adapted.

To reach an adequate number of weapons, an order was sent to Suhl, Thuringia. Once again, only a portion could be delivered, so in 1805 the Bavarian Army received a surprising 28,000 captured Austrian muskets from the French allies. Until 1811 were supplemented though the purchase of Austrian models (M 1798) and alter through newly captured weapons after the victorious 1809 campaign against Austria. So in 1812 the Bavarian Army went to the field with Austrian muskets as their primary weapon.

Standards and Company Guidons (*Kompaniefähnchen*)

During the Napoleonic Wars, the dismounted forces simultaneously had four patterns of standards and various models were in use nest to one another by the regiments. At any given time the current pattern was issued to the regiments and in exchange the old flags were turned in to the arsenal.

During the campaigns from 1805 to 1809 many flags were badly damaged or lost. The model from 1786 was used until 1809. As a replacement the old stocks were used so that further variations were in use at the same time again.

Each regiment initially had a *"Leibfahne"* and three ordinary standards (*Ordinärfahnen*). Starting on 31 March 1804 regiments had only two flags each, so that the 1st battalion carried the *Leibfahne* and the 2nd battalion the ordinary flags, as well as battalion flags[80]. The forces went to the field with this distribution from 1805 until 1812.

Toward the end of the 1812 Russia campaign almost all the flags were lost to Cossacks during a disastrous incident at Uschatsch. During the retreat from Polozk, General Wrede had the flags from the decimated infantry regiments loaded onto wagons for security and brought back with the remaining baggage. On 25 October, on their way, the column was attacked, and the Russian cavalry captured 22 standards[81]!

Only the 13th Infantry Regiment, whose garrison was in Danzig, was able to keep its flags.

The flags cloth had a 170 x 170 cm (5'7'' square) shape. The flagstaffs were lacquered brown. The nails, finials in the shape of a lance head with an open-worked "MJK" royal cypher, starting in 1806, were made of gilded brass. Before 1808 the Bavarian lion was the emblem. The foot of the staff was also gilded. The tassels and cords were silver worked through with blue. The "cravattes" flag ribbons were introduced starting in 1808, and usually dedicated by the commanders. However, before departing for the field, they were removed. These were decorated with inscriptions or floral elements; the mottos read like *"Der Liebe und Freundschaft gewidmet"* ("Dedicated to Love and Friendship") or *"Streitet und sieget fürs Vaterland"* ("Fight and Win for the Fatherland"). The ribbons were adorned with rich gold decorations and fringes.

---

78   For further details and an overview of the models, measurements and calibers, see Hans-Karl Weiss', *Die bayerische Bewaffnung mit dem kleine Gewehr 1800 bis 1815*.

79   He was a French General, who had entered the Bavarian service.

80   Also designated as a regimental flag ("Regimentsfahne").

81   They were displayed in the Kazan Cathedral in St. Petersburg up until the 20th century. See A. J. H(G)ekkel, *Die Trophaen vom Kasaner Dom*, 1909.

The field of the *Leibfahne* was always white and starting in 1808 had the royal coat of arms in the center.

The battalion flag remained unchanged since 1803 and had the blue and white diamond pattern (*Rautenmuster* or *Weckenmuster*). Both of these patterns were the same for all regiments.

In the field the flags were carried and stored in black leather cases.

Virgin Mary's Flag *(Marienfahne) Model 1786*

This pattern served as the *Leibfahne* until 1812, and as the battalion flag only until 1806.

As the *Leibfahne* it had a white field in the center and on a light blue cloud the standing Virgin Mary with a blue cloak over a red dress. The child Jesus is on her arm.

Both are surrounded with a golden halo on their heads. Above them is a white lettered ribbon with gilded lettering. The flag cloth was surrounded by a triple row of blue and white diamonds.

Company Guidons (*Kompanie-Fähnchen*)
Grenadiers 13th LIR, fusiliers 8th LIR, fusiliers 4th Light Battalion

The Presentation of the [captured Austrian] **Trophies 1809.**
Print by Anton Hoffmann in collection of M. Gaertner

Infantry: Flags and Details

Top row: Regimental flag Model 1786, battalion flag
Center: Regimental flag Model 1804,
Bottom row: Gorget 1812, regimental flag Model 1808

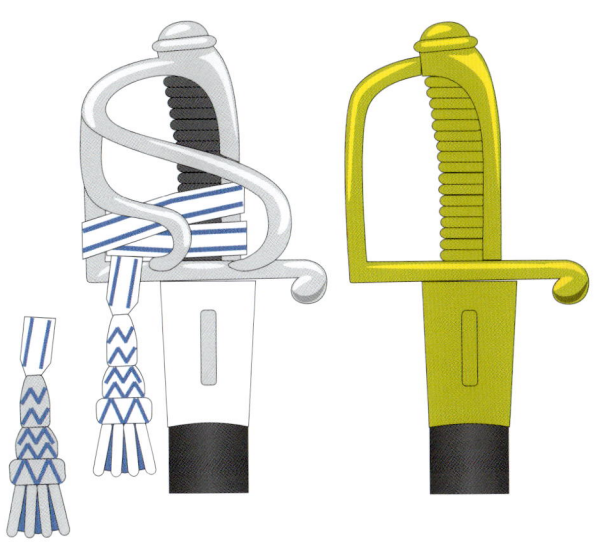
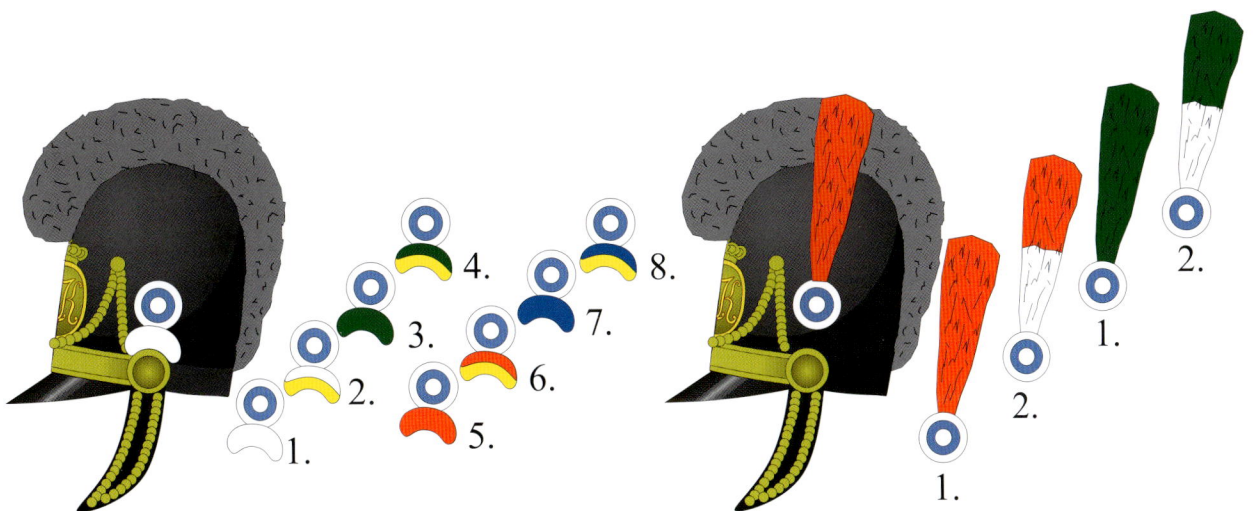

Infantry: Flags and Details

Top row: Kaskett plate, NCO's saber (silver tassel for *Feldwebels*), infantry saber, regimental flag Model 1804, gorget 1812, Regimental flag Model 1808
Bottom row: Kaskett for fusiliers with the company symbols for the 1st to 8th fusilier companies, *Kaskett* for grenadiers and sharpshooters (*Schützen*) with plumes (*Huppen*) for 1st and 2nd.

Model 1803

At the end of 1803 a new *Leibfahne* was introduced that instead of the Virgin Mary now had the coat of arms of the electoral prince embroidered in silk, and a double row of white and blue diamonds border.

The battalion flag's cloth was decorated completely with a horizontal diamond pattern, without any further decoration.

Leibfahne Modell 1806

The electoral prince's coat of arms was replaced by the new royal coat of arms.

Model 1808

For the *Leibfahne*, the center coat of arms was simplified.

The diamond border was dropped, now it was of white cloth with the new State or King's coat of arms in the center.

Distribution of flag model to the regiments in 1812[82]:
- Model 1786: Nos. 6, 10
- Model 1803: the Regiments Nos. 1 and 2
- Model 1808: the Regiments Nos. 3, 4, 5, 11 and 13
- Model 1803 or 1808: Nos. 7, 8 and 9,

Company Guidons (illustration on pg. 69)

These markers for the companies' tent bivouacs were introduced in 1804. They were also used in the field as an aid in orientation when a battalion in column was moving forward. The company guidons were carried by the company's sappers who were at the head of the formation on the march. The guidons were then attached to the handle of the shouldered axe.

The 40 x 40 cm (16″ x 16″) square cloth was divided into two diagonal triangles, which on the staff side was in the color of the line infantry, i.e., cornflower blue, and for the light battalions in green; the other area was in the color of the distinction of the respective regiment or battalion. In the center was a black grenade emblem with the regiment's number for the grenadiers, a black heart-shaped shield for the fusiliers of the Line Infantry with the regiment's number. The edge of the shield and the color of the number corresponded to the regiment's button color. For the light battalions in the center was a red square with the number in button color.

The guidon's point and shoe were brass, although Hess shows iron metal parts in his depiction.

The shaft was black or painted with white and blue diagonal bands.

Differences for the Regiments

13th Infantry - Regt[83]: the flag's field was divided from corner to corner into triangles so that the right and left sides were light blue and the bottom and top triangles were red. In the center was a black circle edged in white with the regiment's number also in white.

The light battalions had no battalion (*Leib-* or *Ordinär-*) flags.

Until 1804, the cavalry carried a *Leibstandarte*. In 1811 only the two converted dragoon regiments still carried their old flags.

Artillery and Transportation (*Fuhrwesen*) had no flags.

Flags of the National Legions 1809

Upon their creation they received flags that were attached to a simple staff with a lance finial.

The flag's silk cloth showed seven horizontal parallel blue und white stripes/diamond patterns.

---

[82] Pierre Charrie, Drapeaux et Etendards, Copernic 1982.

[83] According to Hess's painting, Gefecht bei Wörgl 1809, Residenz München.

REGULATIONS AND ORDERS

Infantry

The predecessors of the printed Infantry Regulations of 1818 and 1822 could be the training instructions by Generals Deroy and Wrede published in May 1804.[84] These instructions consisted of two sections for a school for soldiers and training of or exercises for a company.

Three rates of movement can be recognized from the soldiers' school, i.e., the ordinary pace of 88 steps per minute, the seldom used medium pace 100-104 steps per minute, and the fast pace with 132 steps per minute. All steps should were to be 26 Bavarian *Zoll*[85] long. Loading a firearm took the time to go 18 steps.[86]

The companies included 4 platoons (*Zuege*) and stood in two ranks[87] of 80 men, the excess soldiers being assigned to rear services by the officers and NCOs. The tallest soldiers stood in the first rank; both ranks were sorted from right to left according to the men's body sizes. Each platoon leader (*Zugführer*) stood in the first rank on the right end of the four platoons[88], and the NCO stood behind him in the second rank. The older of the junior lieutenants stood on the left flank of the company in the first rank.

For column formations, the 1804 regulation described the closed and open columns, which supplemented by the so-called *"Contremarsch"* was to guarantee high mobility by the companies.

A bayonet attack was started at a distance of 200 paces from the enemy by transitioning to the fast pace. Only at a distance of 10 to 20 paces and with the order "advance; lower weapon!" (*"Vorwärts fällt's Gewehr!"*) was the soldier allowed to advance individually.

The 20 sharpshooters of each company were dispersed evenly behind the company and commanded by the most senior sergeant. On the command "Sharpshooters, to the front!" (*"Schützen vor!"*), the sharpshooters stepped through the opened gaps between the platoons and took up positions about 8 to 10 paces in front of the first rank in "two-man groups" *"(Zweiergruppen)"*. This "two-man group" was to consist of a forward sharpshooter and a rear sharpshooter, the latter stood one pace behind and one pace to the right of the former. At the command "Sharpshooters advance!) the sharpshooter line went forward and remained about 50 to 80 paces[89] in front of the company. When in march columns the sharpshooters were deployed on the flanks of the company to protect it. For employment in support of more than one company, the battalion's sharpshooters could be consolidated and placed under the command of one or two experienced. The sharpshooters were to be trained in practical exercises, especially running, hovering (*voltigieren*), jumping, wrestling and swimming.[90]

If attacked by cavalry, a company could form a square that consisted of a platoon on each side with the NCOS and sharpshooters standing in the gaps between the platoons.[91]

Shortly before the start of the 1809 campaign, the 9 March 1809 order was reinstate the three-rank battle formation that had been abandoned in 1801. The third rank was formed primarily of sharpshooters who were to load the muskets of both front ranks.[92]

Two companies located next to one another were consolidated to a "division." Thus each field battalion included three divisions or six half divisions (*Halbdivisions*) or 12 "*Pelotons*" or platoons (*Zuege*) or 24 sections or half platoons (*Halbzuege*). Each company accordingly consisted of two platoons of two sections. By detaching the sharpshooter company, the grenadier or carabinier companies created a division by themselves. Platoons (*Pelotons/Zuege*) were numbered from right to left straight through[93] regardless of the companies' numbers. In each company the captain led the first platoon and the senior lieutenant led the second platoon, each in the first rank on the right end of the platoon. The junior lieutenant stood and marched in the middle four paces behind the company's third rank and keep order from there.

---

84 To rehearse the new instructions the existing infantry regiments sent "combined" battalions of one grenadier and four fusilier companies to a training camp at Nymphenburg where they practiced the new drills from 15 to 29 September 1804 and were reviewed by general officers like Hof (see, for example Ruith/Ball or Gerneth, 2. Teil).

85 According to the conversion program on Napoleon Online (http://www.napoleon-online.de/db/bay_masse.php) this corresponds to 0.632 meters [or 2 feet].

86 Firing practice was carried out in accordance with the regulation 1804 at distances of 120, 150, 180 and 210 paces (see Gerneth, 2. Teil, page 7).

87 Gerneth writes that for the period starting in 1801, the infantry "were deployed for exercises and maneuvers in two ranks, for parades in three ranks " (Gerneth, 1. Teil, 1883, page 609). For this deployment for parades, the sharpshooters formed the third rank (Ruith/Ball, 1890, page 153).

88 The first platoon was commanded by the senior lieutenant, the second platoon by the junior sergeant, the third platoon by the second junior lieutenant, and the fourth platoon by the oldest corporal.

89 In the 1804 Nymphenburg (Munich) training ground (Uebungslager) a distance of 150 paces was prescribed (Schubert, page 16).

90 So among others in the 1808 spring exercises of the 6th Line Infantry Regiment (Fabrice, page 151).

91 According the Deroy's 16 September 1806 order, to oppose cavalry, the infantrymen should only shoot at them at a distance of 10 meters or less and use the musket with a fixed bayonet as stabbing weapon (Doederlein, page 103).

92 This tactical formation, ordered shortly before the beginning of the campaign, could not, however be adequately practiced by the troops. So in combat, one was to rely on the "intelligence of the individual leader" ("Intelligenz der einzelnen Führer") (Gerneth, 2. Teil, page 189) to choose whether to employ the practiced two-rank formation or the new three-rank formation. Schubert (pages 131-132) reported the successful exercise in three ranks by the 14th Regiment in a review by Marshal Lefebvre on 27 March 1809, however also the weaknesses of pivoting in the newly decreed six-rank square.

93 So the 1st Field Battalion had, from right to left: the 1st sharpshooter, 2nd sharpshooter, 1st grenadier-, 2nd grenadier-, 1st fusilier-, 2nd fusilier-, 3rd fusilier-, 4th fusilier-, 5th fusilier-, 6th fusilier-, 7th fusilier- and 8th fusilier platoons.

Only in the company on the left flank, was he located in the first rank.

When the second field battalion was alone in the field, the sharpshooter and grenadier company transitioned to the right wing.

After the structural reorganization of 29 April 1811, the infantry formed up in three ranks as long as a platoon[94] was at least ten men strong. If the platoon strength was smaller, they switched to two ranks in order to maintain the front width. The new third rank were to load the weapons of the soldiers in the first and second ranks.[95]

On 24 May 1812, in preparation for the Russian campaign, there were renewed changes to the training instruction, that above all impacted the soldiers' loading and shooting drills and the exact dispositions of the companies, battalions and the regiments.

Regimental commanders issued supplementary and additional instructions that had impacts on the other infantry regiments. Especially worth mentioning was the impact on the 1802 guidance for skirmishers that had been issued by Colonel Graf Reuss of the Leibregiment.[96]

---

94 A half company

95 In the "Training in the Weapons exercises for the Infantry of the Royal Bavarian National Guard 3rd Class in the Isar Region" ("Unterricht in den Waffen-Uebungern fuer die Infanterie der koeniglichen baierischen National-Garde III. Klasse im Isar Kreise")" from 1814 in paragraph 3 (§3) of the tenth chapter an exact description of the shooting process in three ranks: "When firing is conducted in three ranks, the two front ranks fire first (as is always the case for the first two ranks) and as this has happened, the second rank takes the loaded weapon from the third rank, which receives the just-fired weapon and loads it. The exchange of weapons takes place in a manner that after the second rank has raised the fired weapon, and grabbed the weapon with the right hand in the notch of the stock, hand over the weapon with the right hand, and in exchange takes the other weapon and with the left hand grasps it under the third ring."

96 See "Anleitung wie die Mannschaft des Kurfürstlichen Leib-Infanterie-Regiments zum Gefechte in verstreuter Ordnung abgerichtet werden muß. Mit Zeichnungen. Auf Befehl des Herrn Obersten Grafen von Reuß verfaßt von Hauptmann von Brück," 1802, 2 Teile. (see Geschichte Infanterie-Regiment König).

Per the reorganization of 29 April 1811, the companies of a line infantry regiment should deploy as follows.

2nd Field Battalion						1st Field Battalion					
2nd Schützen	2nd Grenadier	8th Fusilier	4th Fusilier	6th Fusilier	2nd Fusilier	7th Fusilier	3rd Fusilier	5th Fusilier	1st Fusilier	1st Grenadier	1st Schützen

Reserve Battalion

12. Füsilier	10. Füsilier	11. Füsilier	9. Füsilier

The light infantry bataillon was deployed as follows:

Field Battalion

4th Füsilier	2nd Fusilier	3rd Fusilier	1st Fusilier	Carabinier	Sharpshooters

Reserve Division

6th Fusilier	5th Fusilier

According to Instructions of 16 April 1803, the six squadrons (*Eskadron*) of a cavalry regiment were consolidated into three divisions (designated by the commanders' ranks). They were deployed in line as follows:

2nd (Oberstleutenant-/Lt. Col's) Division		3rd (Major-) Division		1st (Oberst-/Col's) Division	
Colonel's Squadron	1st Major's Squadron	Rittmeister-Squadron	2nd Major's Squadron	Lt. Colonel's Squadron	Leib-Squadron

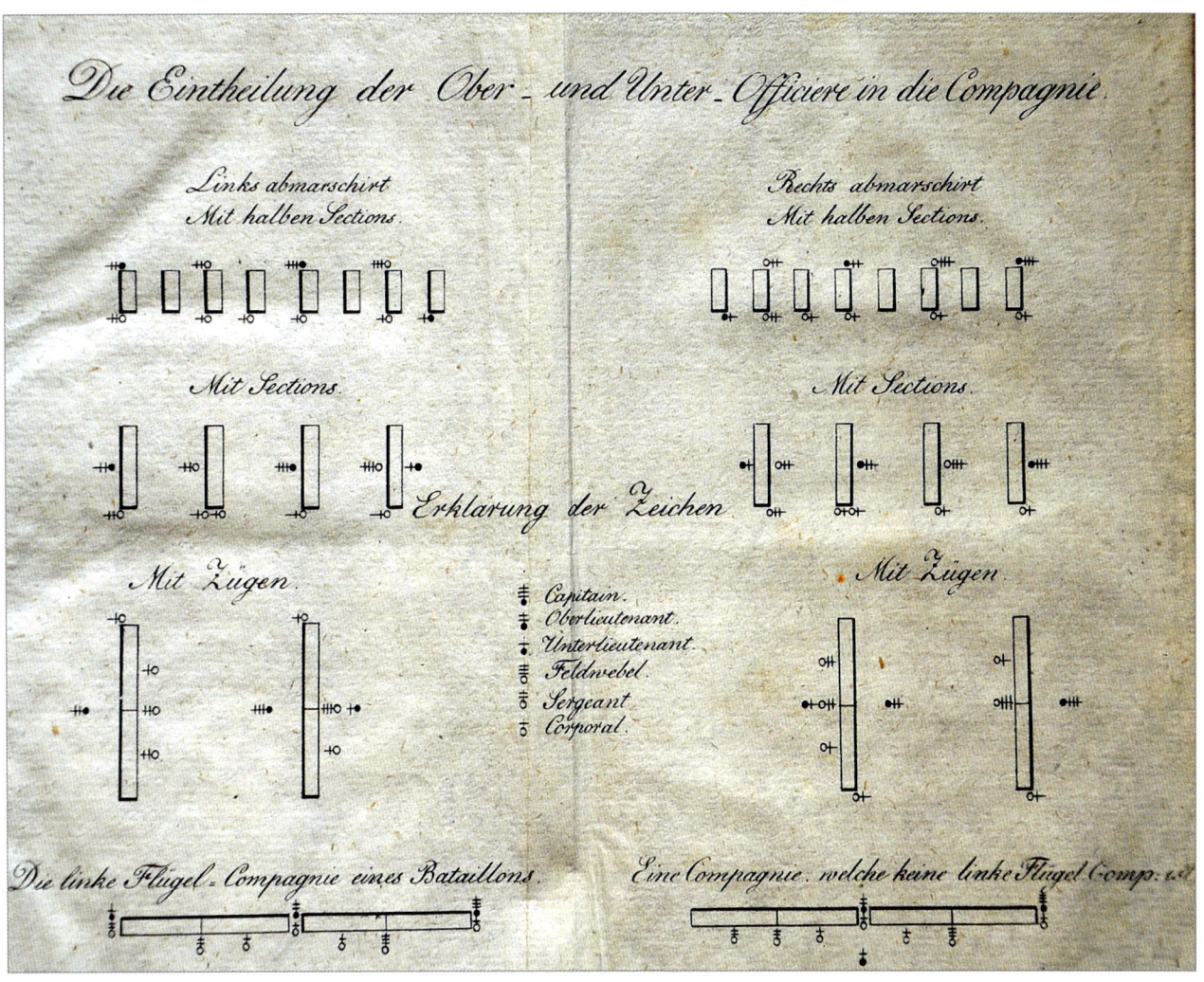

Locations of the Officers and NCOs in the Infantry Companies

(from *"Unterricht in den Waffen-Uebungen für die Infanterie der königlich-bayerischen National-Garde III. Klasse im Isar-Kreise', 1814"*)

From top to bottom, left to right:

Locations of the Officers and NCOs in the Infantry Companies

Marching from the Left with Half Sections

Marching from the Right with Half Sections

With Sections

Explanation of Symbols

With Sections

Captain
Senior Lieutenant
Junior Lieutenant
Feldwebel
Sergeant
Corporal

The Left Wing Company of a Battalion

A Company which is Not the Left Wing

Cavalry

The instructions worked out by Colonel Lindenau in 1802 served as the training regulations for the cavalry.[97] The basic formation for the attack was the line formation that was to be covered by dispersed skirmishers.

The squadrons were arranged in two ranks and an interval of 10 paces between personnel. The second rank stood one pace behind the first rank. According to the 1802 regulation the squadron school anticipated training of columns in platoons[98] or in half-squadrons.

Staying in alignment was not supposed to be done like for the infantry by looking to one's sides, but by the riders' feeling that their knees were touching those of the riders next to them. The gaits of: at a walk, at a trot and at a gallop were not expressly prescribed in the regulation, only "trot and stretched gallop (*karriere*) were to be ridden at such a speed that the laziest or slowest horse can keep up."[99]

In an attack, the first rank should hold the saber ready to strike, and the second rank hold the saber with the arm raised. Yelling in an attack was explicitly prohibited. Loading the carbine, as opposed to the infantry's method multiple steps, took place on the single of order "Load!" (*"Ladt!"*).

When the squadron acted as the advance guard of a force, two cavalrymen were to ride out ahead, and they were followed 200 paces behind by two back-ups. Another 200 paces further back they were followed by an NCO troop, and 300 paces to each side of them, a flank patrol rode. Another 400 paces behind the NCO troop, it was followed by an officers' troop that was also protected by flank patrols. Then 600 paces behind the officers' troop, the squadron followed. It was also protected by flank patrols. The strength of the NCOs' troop and officers' troop depended on the total strength of the squadron. When the squadron formed a rear guard, a similar formation, in reversed form was chosen.

This formation guaranteed that the best-led detachments were placed on the wings and enhanced the cohesion of the cavalry regiment.

With the introduction of the mobile divisions on 22 April 1806, the composition of the three divisions changed henceforth, as the "colonel squadron" (*Oberst-Eskadron*) changed places with the "lieutenant colonel squadron" (*Oberstlieutenant-Eskadron*). Each squadron of a mobile division deployed with 48 men.

Other Branches

In 1803 for duty in the General Staff, Captain Ribaupierre issued a Handbook for General Staff Officers that primarily consisted of translations from the work by Thiebault published in France in 1800.[100]

The King considered the health care of the troops to be very important, so for example, pox immunizations for all soldiers was decreed on 19 April 1807. The service in and structure of Bavarian field hospitals (*Feldspitälern*) was regulated by an instruction of 24 October 1806 and supplementing orders in 1812 and 1813.

Like his predecessor Rumford, Lieutenant General Manson carried out yearly artillery exercises.[101] In the period 1811-1812, an "Instruction for Deployment and Drill of a Battery" (*"Instruction für die Aufstellung und das Exercitium einer Batterie"*). The six cannon were grouped in two half-batteries *(Halbbatterien)* (or "divisions") or in three sections; the two howitzers were positioned on the two wings. An NCO, as gun commander, and 10 men were assigned to each artillery piece. Six ammunition wagons - and the "sausage wagon" *(Wurstwagen)* in the light mounted companies – formed the so-called 1st line *(1. Linie)*, the company's remaining wagons were assigned to the 2nd line or to the Artillery Park.

An instruction from 17 October 1811 governed the independent emplacement of the Artillery and Army Transport Battalion, that artillery officers no longer commanded starting at this time.

The activities of the Engineer Corps was regulated by an instruction that appeared in 1799 on repairing military buildings, supplemented by an instruction published around 1805 on annual inspections to be conducted of military buildings.

---

100 See "Hermes oder Kritisches Jahrbuch der Literatur," Band/Vol. 34, Leipzig 1830, page 320.

101 In these exercises, firing was done at target panels, and accuracy was especially rewarded (F. Münich page 281). Xylander describes an exercise from 1803, in which a 20 meter [22 yards] long and 3.75 meters [12 foot] high wall of targets were fired upon at the ranges of 150, 400 und 600 pace (1. volume, pages 278-279).

---

97 This directive was modified in various ways by diverse orders, but formed the basis for the printed directive from 1828. It is discussed at length in Heinze (pages 281-288).

98 Each half-squadron had two platoons.

99 Heinze, page 285.

DOMESTIC SITUATION

Recruiting and Service Obligations

The decree on recruiting which had been in effect since 11 December 1799 were expanded to all Bavaria's new provinces on 7 January 1805. Within it, all male able-bodied Bavarians[102] between the ages of 16 to 40 were conscripted[103]. The 18-to-38 age group was preferred. The term of service was fixed at 8 peacetime years, and a wartime year counted as two peacetime years.

Minimum heights were specified, for the infantry at least *"5 Fuss 2 Zoll"* in the Rhine measurement system[104], for the dragoons *"5 Fuss 3 Zoll"* (up to 5 *Fuss* 6 *Zoll*), for the chevaulegers *"5 Fuss 4 Zoll"* (up to 5 *Fuss* 5 *Zoll*) and for the artillery *"5 Fuss 4 Zoll"*. Recruits who were small as the prescribed heights could be assigned to either the transportation corps or the internal security forces (National Guard).

The Conscription Law of 29 March 1812[105] established the basis of a universal military service requirement in the active army or in the National Guard. Henceforth no Bavarian was exempt from the military duty requirement[106], while the possibility for voluntary military

---

102 The instruction enumerated a comprehensive list of exceptions for exemptions for military service. Those who did not need to serve, were clerics, the nobility, state officials, court personnel, city citizens with special rights, teachers and professors, doctors, students with character references, apprentices, artists, factory workers and tradesmen. Sole children from both the cities and the countryside were also freed from military obligations. Jews could buy themselves free from military service for 185 Gulden. Other groups were not allowed to buy themselves out of military service.

103 Under conscription, one understands filling the ranks of the army from the (male) population, in which selected age groups had to register and appear at a muster. A set quota of recruits for the army was chosen from the able-bodied men registered as conscripts. During the Napoleonic period, in general these recruits were chosen through a lottery process.

104 According to Döderlein (page 1) this was 1.52 meters (Translator's note 5 feet English/U.S.). Problems with recruiting in times of war led to dismissing these minimum heights, so for example, the 16 June 1807 decree specified only 1.495 Meter (just under 4'11") (Döderlein, page 95).

105 See Königlich-Baierisches Regierungsblatt XXII. Stück, Munich, 8 April 1812, columns 593-700.

106 Only men who were unfit or the sons of families that had already lost several children in the field were exempted from service obligations. Teachers, clergy, rural doctors and students could request a "temporary exemption."

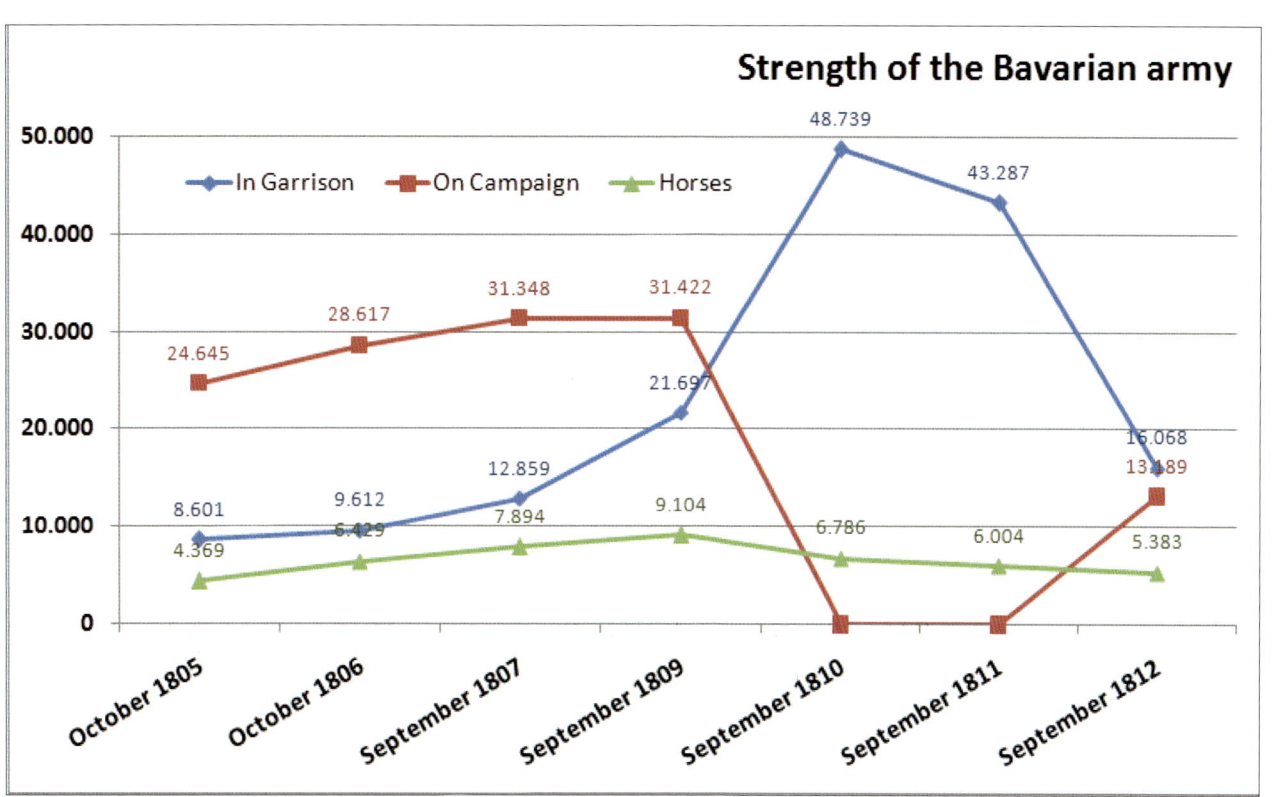

Development of the Strength of the Bavarian Army

service was also offered.[107] The length of service was reduced to six years by this law.

Now all Bavarians from 19 through 23 years old were established as subject to conscription; a minimum height was set at 5 *Fuss* 4 *Zoll*[108]. In contrast to the earlier conscription rules now the units' recruits were drawn from the entire kingdom according to requirements and not as earlier only from specific regions, the so-called "recruiting cantons" (*Rekrutierungskantonen*).

The Conscription Law of 1812 now also allowed the provision of able-bodied substitutes who would perform military duty for the person actually eligible for service. These substitute men were to have an agreed upon amount of money deposited into a bank account. They received the running interest and could have access to the funds after leaving the army.

Eluding military service through self-mutilation or failure to appear or by fleeing could now henceforth be severely punished.[109]

For 1812, 6,000 men born in the years 1790, 1791 and 1792 would be recruited for active service in the army. In 1813, losses from the Russian campaign forced the conscription of 11,513 recruits born in 1794 and 14,548 men born in 1795[110].

For the *Gendarmerie* there was no limitation to the service obligation. *Gendarmes* and NCOs could retirement with a pension starting at age 60 or earlier if ill or wounded.

With the creation of the National Guard 2nd Class with the decree of 6 July 1809, volunteers and all able-bodied unmarried men to the age of 40 could be enlisted. Even former soldiers in the active army could be called into the National Guard 2nd Class. For the National Guard 3rd Class, all male Bavarians to the age of 60 – without exception[111] – could be called up. Married men were assigned to the National Guard 3rd Class.

Officer's commissions could not be purchased like in the old army; henceforth promotions were to be based on achievement on duty.[112] Decisive for this was the 1 January 1811 Army Order, that finally codified promotion would be based on achievement and not longevity. The increase in officer's wages and pensions should be adequate to guarantee material security throughout the period of duty and also make the officer's status attractive for the emerging bourgeoisie and poorer nobility.

The incentive for military service mentioned above was to be established with the pension rules of 1803, 1804 and 1807, independent of the number of completed years of service which established the amount of pension payments.[113] According to these rules, widows of soldiers killed in action received pensions based on the length of service of deceased and could be almost as high the pensions.[114] Additionally to care for the orphans there were the Military Orphans' Fund (*Militär-Waisen-Fond*) established in 1789 and Military Invalids' Fund (*Militär-Invaliden-Fond*) established on 4 March 1813.

Awards and Military Justice

With the founding of the Kingdom of Bavaria, Maximilian Joseph converted the old Military Decoration (*Militaer-Ehrenzeichen*) to the Military Order of Max-Joseph (*Militaer-Max-Joseph-Orden*) on 1 March 1806 (illustration on page 33). The supplementary directive of 23 December 1812 even stipulated that non-nobles recipients of the order could be raised to the hereditary nobility. The Military Order of Max-Joseph was issued in three classes, i.e., Great Cross (*Grosskreuz*), the Commander's (*Kommandeur*) and the Knight's (*Ritter*).[115] The award could only be given to officers who especially distinguished themselves and whose action a neutral observer verified. When the Order was created in 1806, The Great Cross was awarded to six active generals[116], the Commander's Cross on eight active officers, and the Knight's Cross on 49 active offic-

---

107 Volunteers could not only pick the unit in which they wanted to serve, but they could also be favored when applying for promotion to reach NCO status.

108 According to conversion program on Napoleon Online (http://www.napoleon-online.de/db/bay_masse.php) it corresponds to 1.557 meters [5 feet 1 inch].

109 The Army Order of 26 October 1807 set the punishment for self-mutilation as six years imprisonment in peacetime and nine years or the death penalty in wartime (see Gerneth, Teil 2, pages 170-171).

110 Actually a total of 15,653 conscripts born in 1794 were to be called up for duty. However, not that many able-bodied men could be recruited in the entire kingdom, so that now the service obligation had to be expanded to 18 year olds. (F. Münich, page 309).

111 Clergy, doctors and government officials were only excused if they provided a man to replace himself.

112 The shortage of officers fit for field duty was underscored by a 28 October 1805 report to Maximilian-Joseph by Lieutenant General von Deroy about the officer corps of one of his infantry regiments: "The greatest part of the officers are clumsy, idle people, among who many were promoted from the lower class, they are old, fat-bellied and heavy from much beer-drinking, and of a lazy disposition, with long overcoats down to the ankles and far longer broad overcoats, with which the can only drag through the excrement with much personal exertion." (quoted in Gerneth, 2. Teil, page 5).

113 For officers, the range went from 100 Gulden for colonels to 22 Gulden for junior lieutenants; for NCOs and enlisted men from von 7 Gulden 30 Kreuzer for a Feldwebel to 2 Gulden 30 Kreuzer for privates, for the latter the monthly payment if invalided increased to 10 Gulden for Feldwebels to 5 Gulden for senior privates (Gefreite) and privates (Gemeine) (F. Münich, pages 325-327).

114 In any case, the claim for widows' pensions was tied to the established pay rate during the active duty period as specified by the Military Widows Fund established in 1803 (F. Münich, pages 330-332).

115 Recipients of the Great Cross (Grosskreuz) wore it on a ribbon over the right shoulder to the left hip; and the shield from the award was attached to the coat's left breast pocket. Commanders wore the cross around the neck; captains wore the Ritter on the buttonhole (according to Perrot 1821).

116 The Crown Prince of Bavaria, Lieutenant General von Triva, Lieutenant General Graf Ysenburg, Lieutenant General Baron Wrede, Lieutenant General Baron Zweybruecken and Lieutenant General von Deroy. The recipients of the "Kommandeurs- und Ritterkreuze" can be looked up in F. Münich's Beilage (annex) 7 pages 574ff.

Fortress	Period	Bavarian Forces	Losses
Plassenburg at Kulmbach[117]	11 Oct - 25 Nov 1806	13th, later 6th Line Infantry and 22 batteries of siege artillery	1
Glogau	7-25 Nov 1806	2nd and 3rd Chevaulegers and Light Battery Caspers Starting 10 Nov 1806 the 1st Army Division Then relieved by Wuerttemberg Division; Siege artilley remained	39 men
Breslau (ca. 7,000 men, 208 cannon)	15 Nov 1806 - 5 Jan 1807	Cavalry and Light Battery Caspers Starting 8 Dec 1806 the 2nd Army Division Starting 18 Dec 1806 the 1st Army Division	259 men
Brieg (ca. 1,450 men)	8-16 Jan 1807	Brigade Raglovich and Cavalry Brigade Mezanelli Starting 11 Jan1807 Brigade Siebein	18 men
Kosel (ca. 4,200 men)	23 Jan-12 Mar 1807 (partial lifting of the blockade) 12 Mar-18 Jun 1807	1st Army Division and Cavalry Brigade Mezanelli Since 12 Mar 1807 5th Line Infantry, 1st Dragoon and 1 battery Starting 25 Mar 1807 5th and 6th Light Battalion	?
Silberberg (ca. 1,700 men)	27 Jun-3 Jul 1807	1st, 6th and 10th Line Infantry, 1st Dragoon, 2nd Chevaulegers, and 2 batteries	?

The Bavarian forces participated in the sieges above, the casualties mentioned (including officers) also include those from battles with sallying and relief forces.

ers. The 1811 Rank List (*Rangliste von 1811*) mentions the same six recipients of the *Grosskreuz*, and also the eight *Kommandeure*, however now 98 *Ritter* awards.

Starting in 1794, NCOs and troops were awarded the existing Military Meritorious Medal (*Militaer-Verdienstmedaille*) as the award for bravery.

Starting 14 June 1808, soldiers serving in the army who sere not eligible for the Military Order of Max Joseph could be awarded the civilian Meritorious Order (*Verdienstorden*). To provide an award for doctors, on 8 November 1812, the Military Medical Decoration (*Militaer-Sanitaets-Ehrenzeichen*) in gold and silver was created.

Punishments were reduced in the period until 1813[118], so the criminal code (*Halsgerichtsordnung*) which had been in force since the reign of Emperor Charles V was abolished on 16 August 1813. However, running the gauntlet could still be imposed as a punishment[119]. During the entire period, arbitrary punishments by officers or NCOs occurred, but they were severely punished.

---

117 Pierre-Yves Chauvin was able to verify the participation of two Bavarian battalions at the siege of the Plassenburg (castle at Kulmbach) from the memoires of Freiherr von Comeau (Souvenirs de guerres d'Allemagne pendant la Révolution de l'Empire, Paris 1900).

118 In Dauer (pages 170-171), there is a brief description of the military justice system (Militärgerichtsbarkeit) and the soldiers' punishments, and it quotes: "The Electoral Prince is the committed enemy of all physical punishments; therefore no recruit may be struck during his training. In total, one punishes more with arrests, e.g., confinement to quarters, guard duty and the Wasserloch (water hole), of which the last is a very feared punishment. The Wasserloch is a vaulted prison where little or no line enters; usually the prisoner only receives water and bread. In the case of great excesses or frequent offences, caning (Stockstreiche,) on the back or for the infantry furthermore running the gauntlet (Spießruthenlaufen) can be introduced." For further details see Heinze (pages 279-280).

119 It was finally abolished with the Directive of 14 May 1821.

Bavarian Troops at the Assault on Landshut on 21 April 1809
Patrice Courcelle

THE CAMPAIGNS

According to the Confederation of the Rhine Act (*Rheinbundakte*) the Kingdom of Bavaria provided the largest contingent with 30,000 men. However, the strength of the Bavarian Army exceeded this number at times by far as the graphic above makes clear. This table is based on an analysis of the "*Standes- und Diensttabellen der Bayerischen Armee*" (Situation and Service Tables of the Bavarian Army).[120]

During the period of the Confederation of the Rhine, Bavaria was forced to take part in various campaigns on Napoleon's side, namely 1806-07 against Prussia and Russia, 1809 against Austria, 1812 against Russia and 1813 against the Allied Armies from Russia, Prussia, Sweden and later Austria. Bavaria left the Confederation of the Rhine with the Treaty of Ried on 8 October 1813 and joined the Allies' side.

The 1806-07 Campaign

For the campaign against Prussian and Russia, Napoleon demanded Bavaria provide two divisions, however they did not participate in the primary campaign against the Prussian forces in the vicinity of Jena or against the Russian forces in East Prussia and Poland. Napoleon assigned the Bavarian forces the missions of securing the rear areas and lines of communication as well as observing Austria that had been conquered in the 1805 campaign. Thus over the course of the campaign, the role of besieging the Prussian units that had withdrawn into fortresses and preventing their breakouts and reliefs, fell to the Bavarians. These numerous engagements with sometimes small numbers of forces earned the war in Silesia the nickname of the "Lieutenant's War" ("*Leutnantskrieg*").

In 1806, the Bavarian Army was divided into two Army divisions and one Reserve Division, that should each include 10 or 11 infantry battalions, 6 to 8 cavalry squadrons and two to five artillery batteries. The structure in August 1806[121] was as as shown in the table on pages 65-66.

In October, the second division, under acting commander Major General Mezanelli (standing in for the ill General Wrede) initially departed for Saxony and then Silesia, followed later by the first division. The map on page 64 shows the march routes of both divisions for the entire 1806-07 campaign. Both divisions were assigned to the French Army Corps under Jerome Bonaparte.

The beginning of November, the cavalry units of the Bavarian divisions – including the Reserve Division – were pulled together and formed into cavalry brigades analogous to the French Army organization. The first brigade with the 1st Dragoon, 1st Chevauleger and 2nd Chevauleger Regiments was commanded by Major General Count (*Graf*) Mezanelli, the second brigade with the 2nd Dragoons, 3rd Chevaulegers and a Wuerttemberg Regiment of mounted jaegers were subordinate to French General Lefebvre. Count Minucci now took leadership of the second army division, Colonels Lessel and Von Stengelt commanded the division's two brigades.

On 5 January, the 1st and 2nd Bavarian Army Divisions and the Wuerttemberg Division were merged into the 9th Army Corps with its main base being the captured Breslau Fortress.

Due to the departure of the French Grand Armeé toward Prussian Eylau in February 1807, a gap of about 150 kilometers was created between Napoleon's Main Army and the important logistics site at Warsaw. For this reason, an order was issued for the 2nd Bavarian Army Division with a strength of about 7,000 men to move from Breslau (then in Prussia) to Poland. On 8 March 1807, the Bavarians arrived in Warsaw. There Crown Prince Ludwig took over command of the Bavarian forces located in Poland, and starting 4 April, to support Lieutenant General Wrede who was recovering from his illness. With the reinforcements, the Division was reorganized and now included the brigade under Colonel von Pieron with the 4th and 14th Line Infantry Regiments and the Light Battalion Braun, Colonel Lessel's brigade with the 7th and 13th Line Infantry Regiments and the 3rd Light Infantry Battalion as wall as two batteries; General Count Minucci's brigade with the 2nd and 3rd Line Infantry Regiments and the 4th Light Infantry Battalion and one battery; Count Mezanelli's brigade with the 2nd Dragoon and the 3rd Chevauleger Regiments.

After crossing the Bug River at Sierok on 10 May 1807, the Bavarian forces advanced to the Narev River, which they were supposed to cross at Pultusk. On 14 May the crossing took place by four battalions of the 7th and 13th Line Infantry Regiments and of the 3rd Light Infantry Battalion, having driven the Russian units out of their positions. With reinforcement by a battalion of the 3rd Line Regiment and the division's artillery the redoubts at Poplavy were taken. On 16 May, several

Russian brigades with a total strength of about 10,000 men attacked the 3,000 man strong Bavarians at Poplavy. The Russian infantry and cavalry units' attack lasted until about 16:00 hours, when a Bavarian counterattack finally drove the enemy back. The Bavarians' losses were considerable, with 18 officers and 300 men. After the conclusion of the ceasefire, the 1st Army Division under Wrede – the Crown Prince had departed for the Tilsit peace negotiations – moved to the area around Ostrov.

The departure of the 2nd Army Division to Poland led Jerome Bonaparte to decide to order the bulk of the 1st

---

120 F. Münich, Beilage (Enclosure) 9, page 599.

121 Enclosure 2 in Leyh.

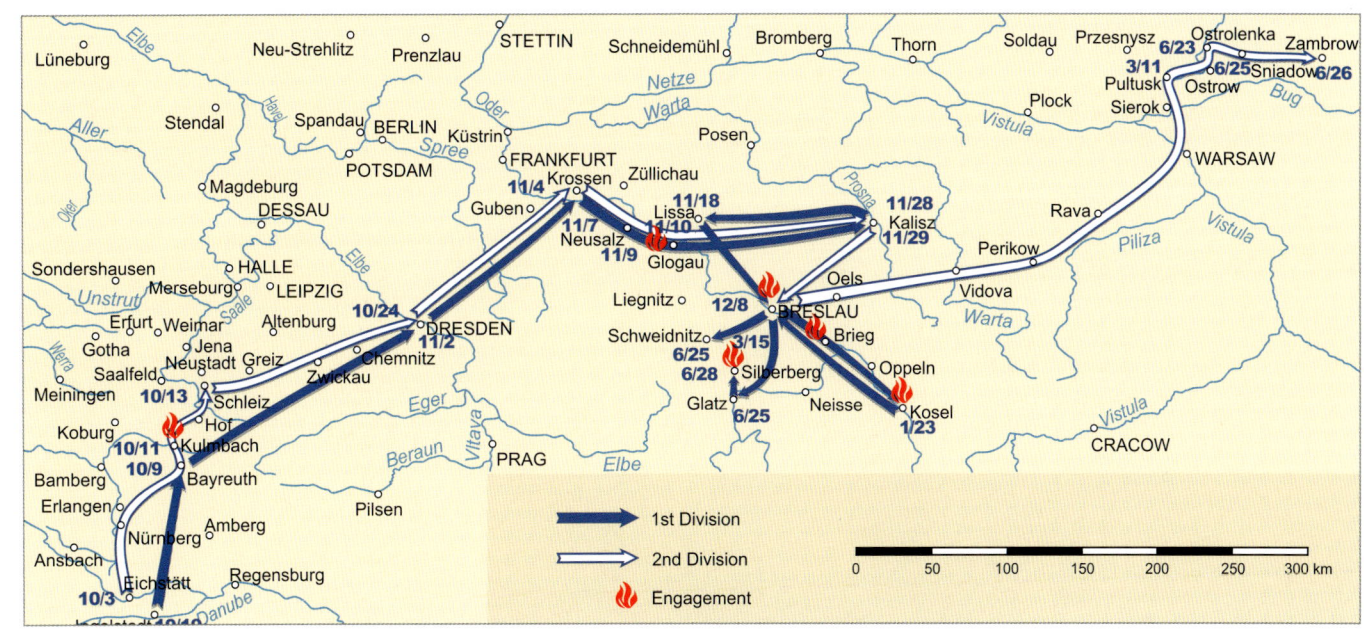

Routes of the Bavarian Divisions in the 1806-1807 Campaign.

Bavarian Army Division, located at Kosel, to move back to Breslau as a mobile reserve. With that, he largely abandoned the blockade of the fortress in the beginning of March 1807.

In mid-March the 9th Army Corps forces in Silesia were arrayed as follows:
- Breslau: 1st Line Infantry Regiment, 2nd Chevauleger Regiment
- Kosel: 5th Line Infantry Regiment, 5th and 6th Light Infantry Battalions, 1st Dragoon Regiment, artillery of the 1st Army Division
- Brieg: 6th Line Infantry Regiment
- Schweidnitz: 10th Line Infantry Regiment
- Neisse and Glogau: Wurttemberg Division

Due to the consolidation of Prussian units under Count (*Graf*) von Goetzen in the Glatz County (*Grafschaft*) Jerome dispatched one after the other the 2nd Chevaulegers, the 6th Light Battalion, the 10th Line Infantry, the 6th Line Infantry, the 1st Dragoons and the 1st Line Infantry. These units took part in the fighting at Nieder-Hannsdorf near Glatz (19 March 1807), Glatz (13 and 17 April 1807), Schoenwalde bei Silberberg (2 May 1807), Kanth[122] at Breslau (14 May 1807), Adelsbach (15 May 1807), Nieder-Eichau (16 May 1807) and Rothwaltersdorf bei Silberberg (4 June 1807) as well as in the storming of the fortified camp at Glatz on 23 and 24 June 1807.

After the conclusion of the Treaty of Tilsit, the 2nd Army Division withdrew to Silesia and took up quarters between Brieg and Breslau in mid-August.[123] The 1st Army Division operating is Silesia was transferred to the area between Berlin and Stettin the end of August.

The beginning of December 1806, the 1st Chevauleger Regiment Kronprinz was detached from the 1st Army Division, consolidated with the French 11th Regiment Chasseurs a Cheval into the Watier Light Cavalry Brigade and assigned to the Grand Armeé's cavalry reserve under Marshal Murat. As part of that unit, the regiment took part in the entire 1807 campaign including the large battles at Eylau and Heilsberg.

---

122 Compare with this the article by Hoesslin about Prussian Major von Losthin's platoon, that appeared in Supplement [*Beiheft*] 10 of the Military Weekly Paper (*Militär-Wochenblatt*) from 1906. In this engagement, one of the 1st Line Infantry Regiment's flags was captured by Prussian forces; one of the regiment's *Fahnenjunker* (ensigns) still had taken the flag from its staff wrapped it around his arm, and while attempting to swim the Weistritz River was killed by a musket ball. As "compensation," in July, Jerome gave the 1st Line Regiment three Prussian flags from the era before 1786, which came from the Glogau (Leyh, pages 97 and 108).

123 On 22 September 1807, Wrede gave a demonstration for French Marshal Mortier with his Bavarian troops of the 2nd Army Division showing the attack by Frederick the Great at Leuthen on 5 December 1757, in which the predecessor units of the 2nd and 7th Line Infantry Regiments had participated.

Lieutenant Kieffer of the Infanterie Leib-Regiment captures an artillery team in the 1806-07 Campaign
Contemporary watercolor, Anne S.K. Brown Military Collection, Providence, USA

Individuals' Heroic Acts

A few examples of personal bravery should be quoted as exemplary for the 1809 Campaign[1]:

Artillery corporal Georg Brunner, from Munich, performed a wonder of bravery at the outbreak of the insurrection in Tirol. When, namely, on 11 April 1809, Major Speicher with his division from Sterzing fought against more than 5,000 insurgents, the cannon that Brunner commanded had all its artillerymen killed or wounded. Ignoring that, by himself he solely kept up a lively fire until he had fired the last round and as a result of a serous wound to his thigh, he sank exhausted to the ground. For this extraordinary act Brunner received the gold *Militaer-Verdienstmedaille* [Military Meritorious Medal].

During the advance to Abensberg against Bach, the sharpshooters of the 1st Battalion of the 14th Infantry Regiment were ordered to cross through the woods to the left of the latter nearby town and to dislodge the enemy dispersed in them. During the advance of the sharpshooters' line, an enemy rider accompanied by three infantrymen, who were attempting to flee, ran into private Georg Hassler from Utzmemmingen. The rider fired his pistol at him and since he missed, he directed several saber blows at him, but did not injure Hassler who parried them with his bayonet and lifted the rider out of his saddle and pulled him to the ground. Thus he gained time to protect himself from the attacking infantrymen by standing with his back to a tree, and they unsuccessfully tried to shoot at him to get him to yield; because they had no way to retreat, they had to surrender to him. For his actions, Hassler received the silver *Militaer-Verdienstmedaille*.

Private Johann Wolf of the Rittmeister "von Romajer" Squadron of the 2nd Dragoon Regiment "Taxis", from Sommerau in the Koetzting district, fought bravely in the combat near Landshut on 16 April 1809. He took an enemy uhlan officer captive after wounding him, but was soon thereafter attacked by enemy riders and surrounded and wounded by three shots. The captive officer used this instant to get free; he also succeeded in wounding Dragoon Wolf's left arm by striking a blow, thus laming him. Wolf, who by no means had lost his presence of mind, took the saber in his left hand, delivered two blows to the officer's face, so that he fell to earth dead, and although Wolf had to be rescued by several rapidly passing by dragoons, he did not relent battling with the enemy dragoons and stabbed three of them from their horses, whereupon the remaining enemies took to their heels. He also freed a dragoon, who had been pulled from his horse. Wolf received the silver *Militaer-Verdienstmedaille* for his demonstrated great bravery.

Private Michael List of the Leib-Eskadron of the 4th Chevauleger Regiment "Bubenhofen" from Zirndorf, in the Fuerth District, performed significant service to his Colonel Ferdinand Baron von Muffel on 21 April 1809 by quick support and notable diligence; then, as the colonel was seriously injured that day, List not only held him so he could remain mounted, but also by tightly grasping his upper arm prevented blood loss and took him a distance to the rear where he lifted him from his horse so a passing surgeon could apply bandages. He had barely laid the colonel down when an enemy cannonball flew over him. List immediately pick up the wounded again and took him to a safe aid station. List received the gold *Militaer-Verdienstmedaille* for his actions.

Corporal Heinrich Sonnleitner of the 10th Infantry Regiment distinguished himself in the battle at Eggmuehl on 22 April, when Lieutenant von Sundahl fell, by immediately taking charge, especially motivating his men, advanced, took the village of Leuchling with levelled bayonets, and thus captured a senior officer and four junior officers and then 80 soldiers. For this exceptional accomplishment, that resulted in the most significant outcomes and the most important advantages for the whole unit, Sonnleitner received the gold *Militaer-Verdienstmedaille*.

During the bombardment of Regensburg on 23 April, Transport soldier Starkmann of the Position Battery Dietrich was wounded in the thigh. He removed the musket ball himself with his bread knife, bandaged himself, and asked for permission to remain with the battery until the firing was completed.

During the march to Salzburg, after the engagement at Neumarkt, Lieutenant and Adjutant Carl Rainprechter of the 7th Infantry Regiment went up on a rise to get oriented. Getting there, he dashed forward alone toward an infantry detachment in a thicket with the cry "Sharpshooters advance," and with this trick forced them to retreat. Scarcely had he done this when he saw several enemy cavalrymen with an officer in the lead, against whom he immediately pounced, took all of them prisoner and additionally captured several horses. Rainprechter received the French Order of the Legion of Honor for this bold act.

When, during the capturing of Salzburg, blowing up the gate did not succeed, Corporal Hummel and the soldiers Anton Kleiber, Anton Dillmann and Foeschler, all from the 6th Light Infantry-Battalion, despite the obvious impending danger, vaulted the wall in order to forcibly open the well-barred gate from within. This bold act, which made possible the rapid pursuit of the enemy, led to the most splendid results. They all received the French Knight's Cross of the Legion of Honor.

In meeting engagement at Woergl on 13 May 1809, artillery Corporal Johann Ziegler of the "Caspers" Battery" from Munich was so badly burned by the igniting of a cartridge box that he had to tear the clothes from his body, whereupon he hurried back to his cannon, without his coat, to continue his duties. For this action, and actually for his demonstrated great initiative on many occasions, Ziegler received the *Militaer-Verdienstmedaille*.

---

[1] Quoted from the works of Heilmann and the Bayerischen Kriegsarchiv "Der Bayerische Soldat im Felde" ("The Bavarian Soldier in the Field" in the Bavarian War Archives).

In May 1807, the forces located on the Inn River, i.e., the 9th Line Infantry Regiment, a light infantry battalion, the 4th Chevauleger Regiment and a battery were consolidated into a brigade under Major General von Vincenti. This unit received the orders to move to the Baltic Sea coast as a covering force, to prevent English or Swedish invasion attempts there. The brigade was incorporated into Marshal Brune's Observation Corps and occupied the cities of Greifswald and Wolgast without a fight. On 10 September 1807, the majority of the Bavarian Brigade moved from Stralsund onto the Ruegen Island and occupied it without any fighting. The Bavarians remained there until 19 November, when the order to march back to Bavaria arrived.

The Bavarian Army's total casualties in the 1806-07 Campaign came to 87 officers and 1,590 men.[124]

The 1809 Campaign

The 1809 campaign was very significant for the Kingdom of Bavaria insofar as it had to resist an offensive by the Austrian Main Army pointed directly at Bavarian territory. Along with that was the insurrection in Tirol, a region that had presented considerable problems since its forced incorporation into Bavaria. This insurrection was distinguished by numerous engagements in this "Small War" ("*Kleiner Krieg*") and was suppressed with a total of three offensives between 9 April and 9 November 1809.

Because of Austria's extensive mobilization efforts, Napoleon had already ordered the Bavarian forces to go to wartime strength in the summer of 1808 and to concentrate the three divisions at Plattling, Augsburg and Nurnberg.

With Napoleon's order of 25 March 1809, the Bavarian Army was supposed to be divided into three divisions each with two infantry brigades and one cavalry brigade, that were to be concentrated in the vicinity around Munich, Landshut and Straubing. The disposition of the Bavarian forces in these three divisions was as follows at the end of March to April 1809:

Commander in Chief of the Bavarian Forces: Marshal Lefebvre (Chief of the General Staff: Divisionsgeneral Drouet d'Erlon)		
1st Division Lieutenant General Crown Prince Ludwig (Chief of the General Staff: Major General von Raglovich) 8,678 men in the Munich area	1st Infantry Brigade Major General Baron Rechberg	1st Line Infantry Regt.
		2nd Line Infantry Regt.
		1st Light Infantry Battalion
	2nd Infantry Brigade Major General Stengel	4th Line Infantry Regt.
		8th Line Infantry Regt.
		3rd Light Infantry Battalion (sent to Tirol)
	Cavalry Brigade Major General Baron Zandt	1st Dragoon Regt.
		1st Chevauleger Regt.
	Artillery Detachment Major Halder	Line Battery Wagner
		Line Battery Hofstetten
		Light Battery Regnier
2nd Division Lieutenant General Baron Wrede (Chief of the General Staff: Colonel von Epplen) 8,938 men in the Straubing area	1st Infantry Brigade Major General Graf Minucci	3rd Line Infantry Regt.
		13th Line Infantry Regt.
		6th Light Infantry Battalion
	2nd Infantry Brigade Major General Graf Beckers	6th Line Infantry Regt.
		7th Line Infantry Regt.
		4th Light Infantry Battalion (sent to Tirol)
	Cavalry Brigade Major General Graf Preysing	2nd Chevauleger Regt.
		3rd Chevauleger Regt.
	Artillery Detachment Major Baron Zoller	Line Battery Dorn
		Line Battery Berchem
		Light Battery Caspers
3rd Division Lieutenant General von Deroy (Chief of the General Staff: Lt. Colonel von Deroy) 9,947 men in the area of Landshut	1st Infantry Brigade Major General von Vincenti	9th Line Infantry Regt.
		10th Line Infantry Regt.
		5th Light Infantry Battalion
	2nd Infantry Brigade Major General von Siebein	5th Line Infantry Regt.
		14th Line Infantry Regt.
		7th Light Infantry Battalion
	Cavalry Brigade Major General Graf Seydewitz	2nd Dragoon Regt.
		4th Chevauleger Regt.
	Artillery Detachment Major Lancy	Line Battery Peters
		Line Battery Roys
		Light Battery Tausch

Together with the forces of the General Staff and the Corps Artillery's three batteries, the Bavarian Army in southern Germany reached a strength of 28,065 men, assigned to 28 battalions, 24½ squadrons and 12 batteries (each with six guns).

At this time in Tirol, consolidated under Lieutenant General Kinkel were: 11th Line Infantry Regiment, 2nd Light Infantry Battalion, 3rd Light Infantry Battalion, 4th Light Infantry Battalion, 2 squadrons of the 1st Dragoon Regiment and a line battery. This totaled 4,450 men in five battalions, two squadrons and one battery of 6 cannon.

---

124 A detailed description by days can be found in Appendix 3 (*Anlage 3*) of Leyh's work.

The storming of the Inn Bridge at Innsbruck, 12 April 1809

Watercolor by J.P. Altmutter, Tiroler Landesmuseum, Innsbruck

On 10 April, three columns of the approximately 120,000 man strong Austrian Main Army crossed the Inn River at Obernberg and Braunau and headed south of the Danube toward Lower Bavaria and Munich. As a result of supply shortages and rain-sodden roads due to continuing rain, the Austrian forces only reached Landshut, which was 80 kilometers away on 16 April. After a fierce fight[125], the 3rd Bavarian Division located there had to withdraw to Pfeffenhausen, toward which the 2nd Division had already rushed to support. Then both divisions withdrew behind the Abens River, where the 1st Bavarian Division that had already withdrawn from Munich, was located.

As Napoleon arrived in Donauworth on 17 April, he recognized the very unfavorable disposition of Marshal Berthier's isolated forces that were in danger of being destroyed. The left wing at Regensburg was formed by Marshal Davout's corps; the right wing, located about 120 kilometers away at Augsburg, was composed of Masséna's corps and Oudinot's corps. Between them, behind the Abens River, were the three Bavarian Divisions under command of Marshal Lefebvre[126]. Napoleon ordered his forces to concentrate by repositioning Davout's corps toward Ingolstadt, Masséna's corps via Aichach to Pfaffenhofen and the Wurttemberger forces under General Vandamme to Ingolstadt.

On 19 April 1809, Archduke Carl, the commander-in-chief of the Austrian forces ordered his three army corps located around Rohr to advance in three columns on Alt-Eglofsheim, Dinzling and Abbach. This movement was intended to isolate and destroy Davout's endangered corps that was marching along the left side of the Danube.[127] However, the Austrian movement happened too late and too far to the right, so Davout escaped the trap and only engaged with the 3rd Army Corps at Hausen and Teugen. On the Austrians' left wing, a brigade under General Thierry with about 5,000 men going from Rohr advanced to Arnhofen, where they ran into portions of the 1st Bavarian Division under Crown Prince Ludwig. In the resulting battle, initially the 2nd Line Infantry Regiment and the 1st Chevauleger Regiment were engaged, and later 3rd and 6th Line Infantry Regiments from the 2nd Division as well. Thierry's brigade was decisively beaten and had to retreat.

As a result of Davout's successful movement, Napoleon could now have a united army of 60,000 men available at Abensberg which now stood opposite Archduke Carl's forces spread across about 50 kilometers between Eggmuehl and Mainburg. Carl now saw that he was obliged to go on the defensive and ordered the 3rd and 4th Army Corps to capture a defensive position at Dinzling and ordered the 5th and 6th Army Corps, located further to the south, to march to the (north) east in order to concentrate his army at Regensburg.

On the morning of 19 April, Napoleon arrived at the location of the Bavarian and Wurttemberger forces around Abensberg and gave a speech that was well

---

125 380 men lost from the 1st Battalion of the 5th Line Infantry Regiment, the 7th Light Infantry Battalion, the 4th Chevauleger Regiment and both foot batteries (Leyh, page 127).

126 Napoleon decided against King Maximilian-Joseph's expressed wishes to have Crown Prince Ludwig as commander-in-chief of the Bavarian forces, and instead appointed French Marshal Lefebvre to command them.

127 Napoleon, in ordering Davout's withdrawal from Regensburg, mistakenly went on the assumption that the majority of the Austrian forces were located north of the Danube, and therefore ordered Davout's forces to march south of the Danube.

received by the troops.[128] On 20 April, the Battle of Abensberg began with the easterly advance of the 1st Bavarian Division and follow-on 3rd Division. Collaborating closely with French Marshal Lanne's newly formed forces on the left wing they threw back portions of the Austrian 2nd and 3rd Army Corps to Rottenburg.[129] In the meantime, the 2nd Bavarian Division under Wrede crossed the Abens River at Biburg and attacked portions of the Austrian 5th Army Corps between Siegenburg and Kirchdorf. The attack here was also successful thanks to the support of a Wuerttemberg brigade and the Austrians retreated to Schweinbach. Around 22:00, Napoleon ordered Wrede to push the Austrians back further, which he accomplished with 2nd Battalion of the 7th Line Infantry Regiment and the 6th Light Infantry Battalion.

The wedge that the Bavarian-Wurttemberg forces drove into the Austrian Main Army at the Battle of Abensberg, now allowed Napoleon to turn to dealing with the enemy's isolated forces. However, going on a faulty assumption that the main part of the Austrians was concentrated at Landshut, he ordered the 2nd Bavarian Division under Wrede in conjunction Lanne's corps, Vandamme's corps and two brigades of Nansouty's Cavalry Division to move in that direction. Both the other Bavarian divisions along with the French Demont Division and a cuirassier brigade were put under the command of Marshal Davout and were supposed to pursue the enemy in the direction of Regensburg. Portions of Masséna's corps marched from Freising via Moosburg toward Landshut.

After the first cavalry engagements in which the Bavarian Zandt Cavalry Brigade participated, the Battle of Landshut slackened on 21 April, during the course of which troops of the 7th Line Infantry Regiments and the 3rd Chevaulegers, under the personal command of Wrede, took part in the capture of the two Landshut bridges about 12 o'clock.[130] In the afternoon, after intense street fighting, Napoleon ordered his forces to actively pursue the retreating Austrians as far as Neumarkt. In this way Napoleon succeeded in completely pushing back the Austrian Army's left wing and he could now turn to dealing with the Main Army under Archduke Carl at Regensburg.

On 21 April, Davout's forces were already advancing in the direction of Regensburg, both Bavarian Divisions moved from the vicinity of Bachl toward Langquaid. During this advance an engagement occurred at Schierling, at which parts of the 3rd Bavarian Division Deroy carried out an artillery duel.

Archduke Carl saw 22 April 1809 as the right time for a counteroffensive, from which the Battle of Eggmuehl developed. To do this, Carl brought the Austrian 2nd Army Corps from Regensburg, but the attack was delayed until midday. This gave Napoleon the time to put his corps located 40 kilometers to the south on the march to Eggmuehl. The 1st Bavarian Division received orders from the corps to advance on Langquaid. The Austrian forces deployed on a line from Abbach to Eggmuehl and prepared for the attack. At the beginning of the battle, the 3rd Bavarian Division was fighting on the left wing, the 1st Bavarian Division on the right wing. The decisive combat took place in the center of the Austrian position north of Eggmuehl at Ober-Laichling, where a battery of 16 cannon rained heavy fire on Napoleon's forces. Therefore, the Bavarian Cavalry Brigade Seydewitz received orders to storm the heights and silence the guns. Together with Wurttemberg and French cavalry, the Brigade finally captured the artillery position after a fierce cavalry melee. Through this, the Austrian's front disintegrated and about 16:00 Napoleon ordered the attack against the entire line.

Archduke Carl recognized the campaign in southern Germany as lost and ordered a withdrawal across the Danube toward Bohemia via Nittenau and Cham. There was fighting at Regensburg on 23 April from which the Austrians were able to withdraw in good order.

Now Napoleon could turn his attention to the Austrian forces' left wing north of the Inn River and ordered the Division Wrede among others to head in the direction of Geisenhausen. The commander of the three Austrian corps, Lieutenant Field Marshal Hiller, had his forces cross the Inn at Neu-Oetting in three columns and march to Neumarkt. On 24 April Wrede made a stand with his division at Neumarkt an der Rott, but had to retreat after

---

128 In the 8th appendix (Anlage 8) of Leyh's work there is a German translation of this speech: "Bayerische Krieger! Ich stehe vor Euch nicht als Kaiser von Frankreich, sondern als Beschützer Eures Vaterlandes und des Rheinbundes. Bavaria! Ihr kämpft heute allein gegen Oesterreicher.
Nicht ein einziger Franzose ist in der ersten Linie, sie befinden sich beim Reservekorps, von dessen Anwesenheit der Feind nichts weiß. Ich setze volles Vertrauen in Eure Tapferkeit. Ich habe bereits die Grenzen Eueres Landes hinausgerückt; ich sehe jetzt, daß ich es noch nicht weit genug getan habe. Ich werde Euch so groß machen, daß Ihr künftig in einem Krieg gegen Oesterreich meines Schutzes nicht mehr bedürft. Seit 2 Jahrhunderten haben die bayerischen Fahnen, unterstützt von Frankreich, heldenmütig gegen Oesterreich gekämpft. Wir werden nach Wien marschieren, wo wir es für alle Uebel, das sie Eurem Vaterlande zugefügt haben, bestrafen werden. Sie wollten Euer Land aufteilen und Euch in die Austrian Regiments einreihen! Bayern! Dieser Krieg soll der letzte sein, den ihr gegen Eure Feinde führt. Greift sie mit dem Bajonett an und vernichtet sie!"
Translator's secondary translation: "Bavarian fighters! I stand before you not as the Emperor of France, but as the protector of your fatherland and the Confederation of the Rhine. Bavaria! You will fight alone against Austrians today.
Not a single Frenchman is in the first line, they are in the Reserve Corps, of whose presence the enemy knows nothing. I have complete faith in your bravery. I have already expanded the borders of your country; now I see that I have not done that far enough yet. I will make you so big that in the future in a war against Austria you will no longer need my protection. For two centuries the Bavarian flags, supported by France, have fought courageously against Austria. We will march to Vienna, where we will punish them for all the ill they have done to your fatherland. They want to split up your land and incorporate you into the Austrian regiments! Bavarians! This war should be the last that you have against your enemies! Attack with the bayonet and destroy them!"

129 About 3,000 to 4,000 Austrians were captured in this engagement (Leyh, page 131).

130 At this time, the Bavarians commanders had halted in the vicinity of a bridge with Napoleon, so that he witnessed Major General Baron Zandt being wounded by a musket ball.

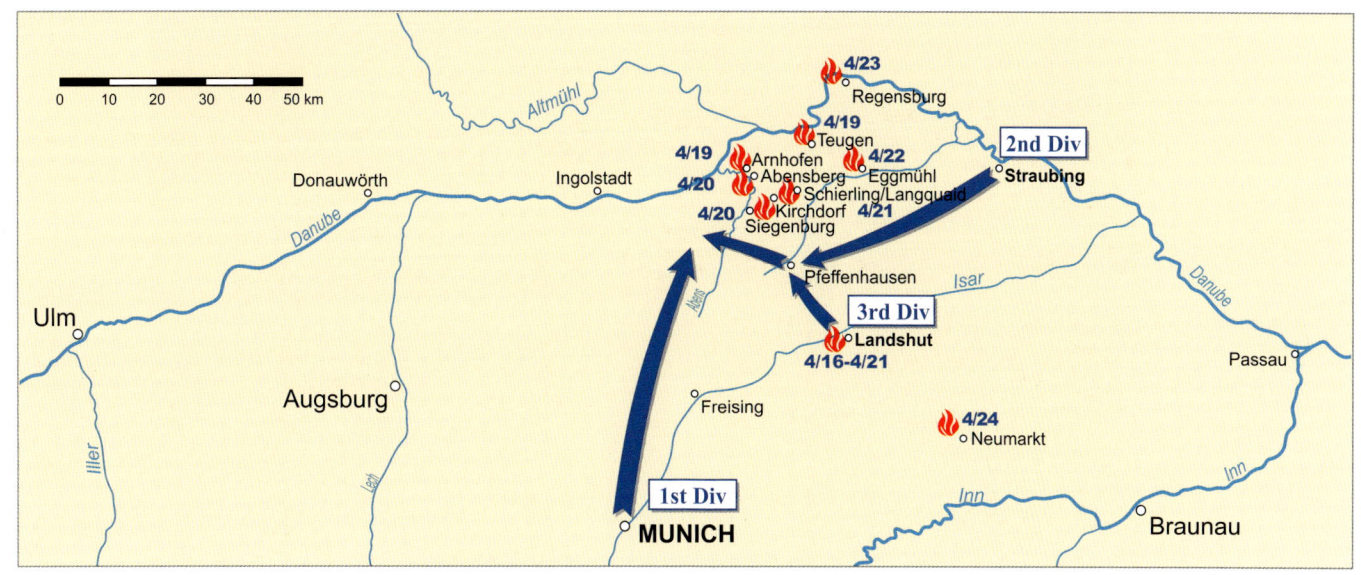

Theater of Operations in the 1809 Campaign

taking heavy losses[131]. As part of Archduke Carl's general withdrawal, Hiller's units also pulled back via Munich. The three Bavarian divisions were given the mission to pursue parts of the Austrian 6th Army Corps toward Salzburg, which they reached after one another on 30 April 1809. With that, the campaign in southern Germany ended and Bavaria was completely free of Austrian units.

Now during the initial pursuit of Archduke Carl toward Vienna, it fell to the Bavarian units to protect the rear area lines of communication and to fight against the Tyrolean insurrection, so that they did not participate in the Battles of Aspern and Essling on 21 and 22 May 1809. In June, the 1st and 2nd Divisions were consolidated in the vicinity of Linz and spent the month in screening engagements. On 30 June, the 2nd Division Wrede, reinforced with 12 cannon from the 1st Division, received orders to do a forced march to Vienna. Up to 6 July, Wrede's forces covered a total distance of 211 kilometers (131 miles) and were still able to come into action on the second day of the Battle of Wagram. Wrede took over the position south of Raasdorf behind French Guards. When Macdonald's assault on the Austrian center resulted in a disarray, Napoleon issued Wrede orders to attack however he saw best.[132] Wrede had his artillery move forward in a line and open fire. Following the firing and advancing cannon were both infantry brigades and following them Preysing's Cavalry Brigade. The Austrian positions were forced back by the effective artillery fire, so the Bavarian infantry and cavalry were only engaged a little. After the Austrian Army's withdrawal, the Bavarian forces slept the night on the battlefield.

Division Wrede joined Marmont's corps that had hardly been employed at Wagram and then took part in the pursuit of the Austrians. On 9 July 1809, the Bavarians ran into the rearguard of the Austrian Army at Staatz. The Cavalry Brigade Preysing successfully attacked an Austrian artillery position there and captured 100 Austrians.[133] On 10 July during the further retreat of the Austrian Army to Znaim, an engagement occurred at Tesswitz, in which Becker's infantry brigade participated in conjunction with French units and suffered heavy losses.[134] After the ceasefire agreement went into effect on 11 July, the Bavarian 2nd Division began its march back to Linz on 13 July where it joined the 1st Division on the 22nd. The 1st Division followed the 3rd Division that had departed five days earlier in the direction of Tirol to take part in the second offensive there. The Division Wrede remained in Linz until the peace agreement was concluded and on 7 October 1809 began its return home to Bavaria.

The campaign against the Austrian Main Army as well as against the rebellious Tyroleans demanded far greater sacrifices from the Kingdom of Bavaria than the earlier campaigns of 1805 and 1806-07 at Napoleon's side. Now not only was it necessary to ready three instead of two

---

131 The nine battalions, four squadrons and 18 cannon crew lost a total of 42 officers and 760 men, according to Leyh.

132 According to Leyh, Napoleon ordered: "Your hour has come, march, attack; act as you best know how to!" (Leyh, page 153).

133 Colonel Floret, commander of the Koenig-Chevaulegers, died from a pistol shot during this fighting.

134 According to Leyh, the 6th and 7th Line Infantry Regiments that were engaged suffered the loss of 47 officers and 850 men.

Portrait of Count (*Graf*) Bernhard Erasmus von Deroy
(11 Dec. 1743 – 23 Aug. 1812)

Individuals' Heroic Acts

The following are some examples of acts in the 1812 Russia campaign in the heroizing style of the 19th Century:

On 26 July 1812, on the march to Vitebsk, the advance guard of Montbruen's mounted corps, to which the Bavarian Chevaulegers regiments under Major General von Preysing belonged, noticed on the other bank of the Duna (*Daugava*) River three riders, who fired at them several times, and one of whom waved a sackcloth (or handkerchief) and yelled loudly. As one, due to the breadth of the river, could neither understood the calls nor differentiate the uniforms, General Montbruen called a halt and inquired, if not one man was present who could swim across the Duna and get information about the three riders. The trumpeter Wilhelm Heligart of the 5th Chevauleger Regiment (Leiningen), born in Mettmann, volunteered for the mission and swam at risk of his life through the raging torrent, induced the hussar officer on the other side, who had a dispatch and verbal orders for General Montbruen, to get in a rudderless boat on the other bank, whereupon in the middle of the distance he himself, noting it was secured to the bank, swam across the river pulling the boat. In this same manner, Heligart brought the orderlies with their swimming horses across the river. The service that Trumpeter Heligart accomplished was of great benefit because the dispatch and the verbal orders were of exceptional importance, and the officer delivering them had, under continuous risk of death, hazarded himself through the enemy. Heligart received, for this exceptionally important accomplishment of duty, undertaken with great personal risk, the golden *Militaer-Verdienstmedaille*.

In the bloody Battle of Polozk on 18 August 1812, the 8th Infantry Regiment (Herzog Pius) under Senior Lieutenant von Storchenau with uncommon defiance of death, despite the enemy canister fire, stormed a Russian battery. Just as the Russian artillerymen raised the match to ignite the canister-loaded cannon, a detachment of these brave men, the Lieutenants Carl Baron Scheben, Joseph Villeneuve, Adam Hebel and Carl von Käfer, then the *Feldwebel* Edlinger, arrived before the muzzle of the gun. At this fateful instant, however, the just as decisive and courageous Sergeant of this good Regiment, Alois Kalkgruber struck the Russian artilleryman with his drawn saber, and severed his hand with the deadly match from his arm. Now the brave regiment took three cannon from the enemy and the carriages and limbers as well. Sergeant Kalkgruber received the French Order of the Legion of Honor for this courageous action.

In the Battle of Polozk, when all of the sharpshooters' buglers were no longer able to fight, the Oboist Nepomuk Betz of the 10th Infantry Regiment was employed for this function, which he fulfilled with perseverance so long that his trumpet was shattered. Oblivious to that, he did not go back, but demonstrated his noble mindedness by not only bringing several helplessly lying officers, who were under withering canister fire, but also used his own clothing to apply bandages thus saving the lives of many a good officer.

On the march to Moscow at Yeraslav on 23 August, a combined advance guard of one half squadron from each the 1st ("vacant") and 2nd Chevauleger ("Taxis") Regiments under the command of *Rittmeisters* (Captain) Joseph Freiherr von Rummel of the 2nd Squadron of the latter regiments ran into a strong detachment of Cossacks and a melee immediately ensued. During the same, Senior Lieutenant Kaspar Willinger of the 4th Squadron of the named regiment fell with his horse; a Cossack officer quickly fell upon him. Right away Trumpeter Joseph Peissner of the 3rd Squadron of the 1st Chevauleger Regiment (from Auerbach, Eschenbach District) sprung to his aid, shot the Russian out of his saddle and helped the Senior Lieutenant back to his feet. A chevauleger who collapsed together with his horse, was surrounded by three or four Cossacks and, already bleeding from several wounds defended himself with his last strength. But our Peissner had his eyes everywhere. Out came his saber! He cut off one enemy's lance; another he struck on the head and the wild fellows disappeared. After returning to the Fatherland, the golden *Militaer-Verdienstmedaille* soon shone on the brave trumpeter's breast.

During the rapidly urged retreat on 21 October 1812, the 4th Light Infantry-Battalion "Theobald" had no more time to call in, in advance, Lieutenant Raphael Bucher who was posted to a mill. The Sharpshooter (*Schuetze*) Ignaz Schoenwetter from the Au suburb near Munich volunteered pass through the enemy and to search for the lost picket and if possible to convey the order to retreat. With luck, he slipped through the enemy and did what he had said. With deliberateness and courage, he then led Bucher and his faithful band in nighttime marches through woods and on byways, driving away individual enemies, back to Rudina safe and sound.

divisions, but the threat on the border and suppressing the Tyrolean insurrection forced the creation of the National Guard and the *Gebirgsschützenkorps* (Mountain Sharpshooter Corps). Since the beginning of the mobilization in June 1808, a total of 24,908 recruits were called up to deal with the hostilities in 1809.[135]

Suppressing the 1809 Tyrolean Insurrection

As already mentioned, one can divide the fighting against the Tyrolean rebellion into three offensives which took place during one half of the year.

The uprising began on 9 April 1809 with the coordinated invasion of South Tirol by Archduke Johann's forces from Austria's Italian regions and the insurrection by the Tyrolean populace under Andreas Hofer. Within a few days the Bavarians were completely driven out of Tirol except for the garrison in the Kufstein fortress and a great number were captured.[136]

In reaction, the 2nd and 3rd Divisions were dispatched to suppress the rebellion in Tirol after their successful campaign in southern Germany. The objective was to retake the Tyrolean capital of Innsbruck. Above all, in the fighting from 11 to 15 May[137], Wrede's second division was able to clear the way against Austrian Archduke Johann's units and the Tyrolean rebels. During the 36-hour ceasefire both Bavarian divisions were able to march into Innsbruck on 19 May 1809. The Austrian forces withdrew again over the Brenner Pass to Italy, and the rebellious Tyroleans also withdrew into South Tirol. With that, (North-) Tirol was again in Bavarian hands and only the 3rd Division Deroy[138] remained as an occupation force.

With the withdrawal of the 2nd Division Wrede, the Tyroleans saw the chance to start the attack on Innsbruck again. On 25 May 1809, about 12,000 Tyroleans attacked the Bavarian outposts outside Innsbruck. On 29 May, Deroy's forces[139] awaited being attacked by 12,000 Tyroleans, reinforced with about 1,300 Austrian soldiers, on the Berg Isel – the so-called Second Berg Isel Engagement (*Zweite Berg Isel Gefecht*). The Bavarian forces got into significant distress during this very costly battle and had to first retreat to Kufstein with heavy losses and then on 2 June withdraw toward Rosenheim.[140]

This emerging danger of Tyrolean forces invading Bavaria by was parried by the 3rd Division - that in the meantime had returned to secure Munich - and the *Gebirgsschützenkorps* (Mountain Sharpshooter Corps) raised and commanded by Count Arco. It was possible to fend off the attack and in June 1809 to permanently secure the Kufstein Fortress.

After the departure of the bulk of Deroy's division toward Linz ordered by Napoleon, it reached the city on 12 July, leaving the defense of Kufstein to the few remaining troops and Count Arco's corps[141]. Due to the ceasefire agreed to by Archduke Carl, Napoleon was able to turn his attention to putting down the Tyrolean uprising. A final victory was supposed to be achieved by an attack from the east through the Pusta Valley by Wurttemberg forces (also putting down a rebellion in the Vorarlberg region) and French forces under General Rusca, coordinated with a central main attack between Salzburg and Mittenwald by the Bavarian 1st and 3rd Divisions, the Arco "Corps" and the Division Rouyer[142] under General Lefebvre.

The advance began the end of July 1809, and after eight days, the forces were concentrated around Innsbruck. Marshal Lefebvre let himself be induced from taking the simple march route from Innsbruck immediately further in the direction of South Tirol. Division Rouyer moved out, however, on 4-5 August met with bitter resistance at Oberau in the so-called "*Sachsenklemme*" ("Saxon Trap") valley and suffered heavy losses[143] and had to withdraw. Thereupon, Lefebvre advanced with the 1st Division and parts of the 3rd Division and attempted to advance in the direction of Brixen and Meran. In any case the units he dispatched found themselves in numerous ambushes[144] by Tyrolean farmers who made clever use the valleys' terrain, so that Lefebvre ordered a retreat to Innsbruck. This retreat was marked by further fierce attacks by the Tyrolean farmers on the slopes; but the forces reached Innsbruck on 11 August 1809. On 13 August, Andreas Hofer gathered about 18,000 men and attacked Innsbruck in three columns in the Third Berg Isel Engagement, but was not able to overcome the Bavarian defense. Despite the

---

135 Leyh indicates that for a total population of about two million inhabitants, reaching more than 1% recruiting proportion would be "a considerable achievement for conditions at that time. (Leyh, page 182). In the overview of the Confederation of the Rhine countries (Übersicht der Rheinbundstaaten) published in Napoleon Online (see http://www.napoleon-online.de/armee_rheinbundstaaten.html), for 1810 a total of 3.5 million inhabitants is mentioned.

136 Along with losing about 500 dead and wounded, 3,350 men were captured by the Tyroleans, as were six cannon and two flags. Among the dead was also the commander of the 11th Line Infantry Regiment, Colonel von Dietfurth (Leyh, page 143).

137 Division Wrede's fighting on 13 May 1809 at Woergl (the First Berg Isel Engagement) should be especially highlighted, because they were victorious over the Austrian forces under Chasteler and their own losses of 191 men as compared to about 3,000 prisoners, 9 captured cannon and three captured flags. (Translator's Note: The Isel Mountain is located just outside Innsbruck.)

138 With the 5th, 9th and 14th Line Infantry Regiments, the 7th Light Infantry Battalion, the 2nd Dragoon Regiment and a battery, it was about 4,200 men all taken together (Leyh, page 156).

139 In the meantime reinforced by the 10th Line Infantry Regiment.

140 At the Battle of Berg Isel the Bavarians lost 209 men; in the retreat another 165 men (Leyh, page 158).

141 Consisting of the Gebirgsschützenkorps (Mountain Sharpshooter Corps) and five of the six reserve battalions that had been raised in the meantime.

142 Consisting of seven battalions of Confederation of the Rhine forces from Anhalt, Lippe, Schwarzburg, Waldeck, and Reuss, as well as the Bavarian 4th Chevaulegers and a Bavarian battery.

143 About 1,000 men died, were wounded or captured.

144 At the fighting on 8 August 1809, the 10th Line Infantry Regiment and the 2nd Dragoon Regiment lost a total of 1,098 men and four cannon. After that, the 10th Regiment could only provide 19 officers and about 300 men.

Route of the Bavarian Forces in the 1812 Campaign

successful resistance, Lefebvre ordered the withdrawal from Tirol, which was completed in mid-August.

After the fighting around Salzburg, where the Bavarian 1st Division and Rouyer's Confederation of the Rhine forces were stationed, the third offense to take Innsbruck was supposed to begin in October 1809. Napoleon relieved Lefebvre of command of the Bavarian forces and handed it over to Drouet d'Erlon. Together with Eugène Beauharnais, who was advancing from Italy and Carinthia with five divisions, they were to finally defeat the rebellion.

The three Bavarian divisions were united on 24 October in the Inn Valley (*Inntal*), and were able to march into Innsbruck again on 1 November 1809. There, at the Fourth Berg Isel engagement, the Bavarian 2nd Division under Wrede was able to shoot up the Tyrolean positions by having its artillery precede its infantry as it did at the Battle of Wagram.[145]

With the victory at Berg Isel and the capture of the city of Bozen, Eugène Beauharnais' forces, the resistance by the Tyrolean rebels was broken for good. On 9 November 1809, Andreas Hofer published a manifesto in Sterzing in which he called on his countrymen to cease further armed resistance. After a few further incidents, Tirol could be occupied. At the end of 1809, the 1st Division was located in the upper Inn valley (*Oberinntal*), the 2nd Division around Innsbruck and the 3rd Division in the Inn valley between Imst and Rattenberg.

The 1812 Campaign

On 11 December 1811, the Kingdom of Bavaria was issued Napoleon's order to mobilize its forces for the planned campaign against Russia. For the campaign, Bavaria was to provide two divisions each with three infantry brigades with five battalions each, one cavalry brigade with three regiments, two mounted and three foot batteries with six cannon each.

The units of the 1st Division ordered to Danzig were later assigned to Marshal MacDonald's 10th Army Corps.

In March 1812, both divisions marched through Saxony, then through Silesia to Poland and via East Prussia to the Neman River where they occupied their assigned area in preparation for the invasion. At the end of March, the 1st and 2nd Chevaulegers were detached from the Bavarian command and merged with the Saxon Prinz Clemens Chevauleger Regiment into the 17th Cavalry Brigade of the 3rd Cavalry Corps under General Grouchy.

The Bavarian forces subordinate to the 6th Army Corps were consolidated with the Italian 4th Army Corps under Eugène Beauharnais. After crossing the Neman on 2 and 4 July, they followed Napoleon's Main Army that was already advancing. After a seven-day rest phase in the vicinity of Anuschischki, the Bavarians received orders on 12 July 1812 to detach from the 4th Army Corps and to follow the Main Army to Vilnius. They reached that city on 13 and 14 July, where Napoleon personally reviewed

---

145 *Thus several hundred Tyroleans were taken prisoner and five cannon and one flag were captured; their own losses were 41 men (Leyh, page 172).*

the Bavarian forces.[146] The Emperor Napoleon was especially taken with the Bavarian cavalry and artillery and now pulled the four remaining Chevauleger regiments and the 1st Light Battery out of the 6th Army Corps and assigned them to Count Preysing's command as a cavalry division in the 4th Army Corps. As a result, the Bavarian forces were completely without cavalry and were disadvantaged by more difficulties with reconnaissance, but also heir possibilities for supplying their troops were clearly handicapped.

During their march to Vitebsk, the Bavarians received orders to head turn northwest to Polozk – a city on the Duna River with about 12,000 inhabitants at that time – to come to the aid of Marshal Oudinot's 2nd Army Corps which was threatened by Russian forces under General Wittgenstein. They reached the area of Polozk on 7 August 1812 with a strength already reduced to about 10,000 men[147] and would not leave this area again for about three months. The 2nd and 6th Army Corps, now combined, were put under the command of Marshal Oudinot.

The forces, with a total of 863 officers and 28,000 men in 30 battalions and 24 squadrons, were organized in two divisions as follows:

6th Corps of the Grand Armeé, Marshal of the Cuirassiers Count Gouvion St.-Cyr (Chief of the General Staff Colonel d'Albignac, Artillery: Colonel of Artillery von Colonge)		
1st Division (19th Division) Infantry General von Deroy (Chief of the General Staff: Major von Gravenreuth) 356 officers, 11,378 men, 2,389 horses, 24 cannon	1st Infantry Brigade Major General von Siebein	1st Light Infantry Battalion
		1st Line Infantry Regt.
		9th Line Infantry Regt.
	2nd Infantry Brigade Major General von Raglovich	3rd Light Infantry Battalion
		4th Line Infantry Regt.
		10th Line Infantry Regt.
	3rd Infantry Brigade Major General Graf Rechberg	6th Light Infantry Battalion
		8th Line Infantry Regt.
		13th Line Infantry Regt. (send to Danzig)
	1st Cavalry Brigade Major General Graf Seydewitz	1st Chevauleger Regt.
		3rd Chevauleger Regt.
		6th Chevauleger Regt.
	Artillery Detachment Colonel Freiherr von Lamey	1st Light Battery
		3rd Light Battery
		1st Line Battery
		2nd Line Battery (sent to Danzig)
		6th Line Battery (12-Pounder)

2nd Division (20th Division) General of Cavalry Graf von Wrede (Chief of the General Staff: Colonel von Comeau) 397 officers, 12.795 men, 3.498 horses, 30 cannons	1st Infantry Brigade Major General von Vincenti	2nd Light Infantry Battalion
		2nd Line Infantry Regt.
		6th Line Infantry Regt.
	2nd Infantry Brigade Major General Graf Beckers	4th Light Infantry Battalion
		3rd Line Infantry Regt.
		7th Line Infantry Regt.
	3rd Infantry Brigade Major General Graf Minucci	5th Light Infantry Battalion
		5th Line Infantry Regt.
		11th Line Infantry Regt.
	2nd Cavalry Brigade Generalmajor Graf Preysing	2nd Chevauleger Regt.
		4th Chevauleger Regt.
		5th Chevauleger Regt.
	Artillery Detachment Colonel von Zoller	2nd Light Battery
		4th Light Battery
		4th Line Battery (12-Pounder)
		5th Line Battery
		8th Line Battery

In the period from 7 to 14 August, the Bavarian Corps was engaged in numerous long exhausting marches and minor skirmishes northwest of Polozk. On the afternoon of 16 August, the 2nd and 6th Army Corps were back in Polozk. The only result of the marches was a reduction of the Bavarians from 16,000 to 12,500 effective fighting men.

Wittgenstein followed the retreating Bavarians and attacked them on 16 August about 14:00 outside Polozk. The Bavarians repulsed this Russian attack as well as a second one three hours later. That evening, Marshal

---

146 In Deroy's report of 19 July 1812, to the King of Bavaria, he described the surprising parade on 13 July: "In the afternoon, as I paid my respects to the Major General [Authors: Marshal Berthier], I heard that there would be a review already on the next day, and that evening suddenly about 6:30, General St. Cyr came alone into my quarters and informed me that the emperor had also ridden into the camp. While we hurriedly rode after him, the emperor first came to the 2nd Inf. Bde. Because the people did not have time to properly get dressed and get their weapons, they lined up in field caps and "chemises" (shirts) [Leyh's comment: the overcoats were called chemises at that time] and received his majesty with 'Vive l'Empereur!' The emperor then rode to the cavalry [brigade] and the 2nd and 3rd Inf. Brigades and seemed very satisfied with the speed with which the troops had assembled and the kind of reception." (Quoted in Leyh, page 199).

147 On 11 August, Deroy reported that now only about 16,000 men at Polozk "arrived in a spirit of despondence, faint-heartedness, indignation, unruliness and insubordination." (Quoted in Leyh, pages 200-201).

Oudinot held a council of war with his generals during which they agreed on the disposition for the allies for 17 August. The 8th French Division was located on the left wing. To the right of it in the center on the road to St. Petersburg were the 6th Division made up of French and Portuguese troops. The right flank would be held by Wrede's 20th Division that would be take up a fortified position in the village of Spas with Vincenti Brigade. Deroy's 19th Division was located behind Wrede on the heights south of the Polota River. The 9th Swiss Division, the cavalry of the 2nd Army Corps and the artillery reserve including the Bavarian 12-pounder-batteries were located south of the Duna River.

Between 7 and 8 o'clock on 17 August, the 1st Russian Corps attacked with about 25,000 men under General Wittgenstein. The Bavarian Division Wrede was assigned a key position in the fortified village of Spas northeast of Polozk that they were able to defend with great effort against the numerically superior Russians. The Deroy Division was held back as the reserve. The main burden of the fighting around Spas was born by the Bavarian 1st and 3rd Brigades. The 2nd Brigade was located on the extreme right wing and did not get engaged in the fighting. By bitter fighting with multiple bayonet charges and counterattacks, the Bavarians were able, with heavy casualties, to ward off the Russian attacks.[148]

On the following day, a surprise attack by the French-Bavarian forces under General St.-Cyr[149] were to take place from the defensive position at Polozk. At about 16:00, the battle was initiated with a heavy artillery bombardment of the Russian bivouac locations. Shortly thereafter the Bavarians attack on the surprised Russians. Count Becker's 2nd Brigade from Wrede's division led the attack, to the right next to Deroy's 2nd (Raglovich) Brigade. The Russians recovered quickly from the surprise of the counterattack and received the Bavarians with heavy infantry fire[150] the Bavarians thereupon went back and were in danger of being flanked by the Russians. Thanks to the 7th and the 4th Line Infantry Regiment, the Russians could be driven back.[151] General Wrede gathered the Bavarian forces and led them forward in a counterattack. The 9th Line Infantry Regiment ejected the Russians from the Prismenitza palace (north of Spas)

Carl Philipp Joseph von Wrede
(29 April 1767 – 12 December 1838)
Bavarian Field Marshal and Diplomat

with hand-to-hand fighting. With the loss of Prismenitza, the battle was lost for the Russians. Wittgenstein ordered a withdrawal.

After the last fighting during the withdrawal, in which the Bavarian artillery and the 1st Battalion of the 1st Line Infantry Regiments also participated, the first Battle of Polozk ended about 21:30.

The success on 18 August 1812 was overshadowed by the Bavarians' heavy losses; they lost a total of 15 dead and 103 wounded officers and 129 dead and 1,032 wounded soldiers.[152]

To perform reconnaissance, an approximately 1,800 man Bavarian detachment under General von Siebein was to advance on the road to St. Petersburg on 22 August. At Bielaia they ran into a strong enemy rearguard that attacked the Bavarians with superior numbers. During the engagement, Major General von Siebein was mortally wounded, and Colonel von Stroehl of the 1st Line Infantry Regiment became his successor. He was able to hold this position until 24 August, on which day the retreat to Polozk occurred.

---

148 Both Bavarian brigades lost a total of 465 men; among the wounded was Brigadier General Vincenti, who gave over command of the brigade to Colonel Graf (Count) Spaur of the 2nd Line Infantry Regiment (Leyh, page 206).

149 He replaced the wounded Marshal Oudinot as commander-in-chief of both Army Corps.

150 The Russian's strong defense then was also benefited by the poorly coordinated deployment of the Raglovich Brigade. The Infantry companies had to maneuver by sections through a built up area and then form up again opposite the Russians. In a short time in the following intense firefight, Major General Raglovich, Colonel Count/Graf Preysing of the 10th Line Infantry Regiment and Lieutenant Colonel Bernclau of the 3rd Light Infantry Battalion were wounded (Leyh, pages 207-208).

151 During this critical phase of the battle, General von Deroy was seriously wounded by a musket ball to his lower abdomen. General Saint-Cyr thereupon put General Wrede in command of the Bavarian 1st Division as well.

152 The importance of the actions of the Bavarian forces during the two days of fighting at Polozk is underscored by the 60 Crosses of the Legion of Honor bestowed among them by Napoleon (Leyh, page 209).

In the following quiet phase, the remainder of both Army Corps took up fortified positions in and around Polozk. The poor sanitary conditions and the shortages of supplies further reduced the fighting strength of the Bavarian unit[153] that only had a total of 6,800 able-bodied men available on 29 August.

Russian General Wittgenstein had in the meantime until mid-October assembled around 50,000 men and 175 cannon and was supposed to attack the Grand Armeé's line of retreat and then advance to the Berezina River. After the first encounter with the Bavarian forces under General von Stroehl at Drizna on 16 October 1812, the second Battle of Polozk took place on 18 October. The Bavarians were located in the second line in two redoubts and, after the Russian attackers' success against the first French line, were able to repulse the Russians with heavy artillery fire.

On 19 and 20 October, Wrede, whom St. Cyr had entrusted with defending against the Russian efforts, was able to prevent Wittgenstein's attempted flanking of the opposing forces west of Polozk at the Uschatz River. Saint-Cyr had already ordered the withdrawal from Polozk, so on 22 October 1812 the about 3,800 remaining Bavarians together with the French Corbineau Cavalry Brigade fell in to march back from Rudnia.

Initially Wrede marched westerly, separated from the remaining forces of the former 2nd Army Corps, then made a hook to the south, and then west again to orient toward Danilovitschi. The Bavarians arrived there on 29 October and remained there until 28 November 1812. During this retrograde march, Wrede sent the Bavarians' war chest with a few baggage wagons and the Infantry regiments' 22 standards, with weak escort, followed by one and one-half batteries, via Uschatz to Kublitschi. A Russian patrol was able to stop the convoy and capture the Bavarian standards along with the war chest.[154]

In Danilowitschi the badly decimated battalions were reorganized into (combined) companies, so Wrede now had available 20 companies each with about 100 men.

On 8 November, the Corbineau Cavalry Brigade, which had been marching with the Bavarians, was detached to support the retreat of the remains of the Grand Armeé over Berezina.

Using convalescent troops and reinforcements arriving from Bavaria, the Bavarian Corps was brought up to 27 companies with 24 cannon again. With the arrival of reinforcements[155] from Vilnius n mid-November, Wrede again had nearly 10,000 men at his disposal.

He began the march to Glubokoye on 16 November 1812, but stopped his eastward movement because of the Russian pincer movement[156] on the Berezina, and turned toward Dogschitzi/Dokshytsy. Wrede remained there until 29 November[157] and then marched to Vileyka per Marshal Berthier's orders. On 4 December, the Bavarian forces had to fend off several Russian attacks and were able to withdraw with units in good order that evening. On 6 December, they crossed the Vilya River on the thick ice with the remaining cannon and continued the retreat toward Vilnius.

On the night of 9 December 1812 in Kiena, Wrede received Berthier's orders to march with the remaining circa 1,000 able-bodied soldiers[158] to Rukoni, to allow Marshal Victor's 9th Army Corps to pass through and then take over the rear guard of the whole army under the command of Marshal Ney. Russian forces blocked Wrede's entry into Vilnius, so he had the entire corps form a square and march, fighting in this formation to the outskirts of Vilnius. Having arrived there, any semblance of order was lost, but Wrede and some officers were able to assemble a small Bavarian force of bout 300 men and 30 Chevaulegers.

The rear guard with the Bavarians[159] departed Vilnius on 10 December 1812 and crossed the iced-over Ponary Mountain, where the last 15 Bavarian cannon had to be left behind. On 11 December at Zizmory, an engagement with Russian infantry and artillery took place, in the course of which the e two Bavarian companies got separated.[160] On 14 December, the remainder of Wrede's forces united with about 1,200 advancing men, who then marched together to the Vistula unmolested by Cossack attacks that had now ceased.[161] [162]

The cavalry regiments that had been separated from the Bavarian divisions early in the campaign marched in their units on the main line of advance in the direction of Moscow. There are no major actions to mention for the cavalry up until the Battle of Borodino, so they had no significant losses of personnel. In any case, the Chevaulegers lost many horse that died dung the long march and from emaciation due to inadequate feed.

---

153 The highest-ranking Bavarian medical officer, Oberstabsmedicus Koehler, reported that for September 1812 of a daily increase of 150-180 sick in the dispensaries and a daily death rate of 20-30 men (quoted in Leyh, page 212).

154 These flags were taken to St. Petersburg and hung as trophies in the Kazan Church (Leyh, page 246).

155 Two columns from Marshal Victor's forces, among them especially Westphalian and Hessian units (Leyh, page 247).

156 Wittgenstein's army coming from the north and Tschitschagov's army from the south.

157 Due to the significant fall in temperature during these days – on 13 November the first heavy frost arrived, later the temperature sunk to minus 18 degrees Celsius – Wrede's reinforced forces suffered heavy losses again from sickness and freezing.

158 According to Leyh only those remaining from Bavaria, Westphalia and Hessen (page 251).

159 Each of both divisions formed only one company.

160 The company from the 1st Division was cut off from its line of retreat and on 20 December 1812 and the Russians captured its 20 officers and 20 men. The company from the 2nd Division reached the Neman River on 13 December with 68 men (Leyh, page 252).

161 During this march, three columns of reinforcements with a total of 4,200 men reached Wrede's Army Group.

162 The 3rd, 4th, 5th and 6th Chevaulegers Regiments and the 1st Light Battery Wiedenmann. During this cavalry engagement, the Preysing Division lost a total of five officers, 62 men and 82 horses (Leyh, page 229).

The Bavarian Corps at the Battle of Polozk, 17 and 18 August 1812
Colored engraving at Friedrich Campe, Nuremberg
Anne S.K. Brown Military Collection, Providence, USA

During the Battle of Borodino on 7 September 1812, the Preysing Cavalry Division was busy on the left flank of Napoleon's army protecting against the major attack by the Russian 1st Cavalry Corps under Uvarov and Platov's Cossacks. After defending against the Russian cavalry attack, the commander on the left wing of the French Army, Eugène Beauharnais, wanted to secure the Rayevsky redoubt that in the meantime had been captured in the meantime by units from Grouchy's cavalry corps. The 1st and 2nd Chevaulegers who had consolidated there were immediately attacked by Russian cavalry and taken under fire by infantry. Their participation on the last futile attack by Grouchy's cavalry corps decimated both Bavarian regiments even further.[163]

The Bavarian Chevaulegers advanced toward Moscow with the other units of the Grand Armeé. The Preysing Cavalry Division, which now only consisted of 700 to 800 horsemen, vacated the camps around Moscow on 22 September 1812 and went back on the road to Smolensk to secure the rear lines of communication. The badly decimated 1st and 2nd Chevaulegers[164] also departed with Grouchy's Cavalry Corps on 21 September and reached Tarutino the beginning of October.

On 18 October, even before the beginning of the general retreat, the Preysing Cavalry Division with the battery and the 3rd and 6th Chevauleger Regiments[165] had to fend off an attack by six Russian cavalry regiments at Masikova On the way to Malo-Yaroslavetz the

---

163 On the evening of 7 September, both regiments could only count 180 riders who were consolidated into two squadrons and put under the highest-ranking able-bodied officer, Major Freiherr von Lerchenfeld. During the fighting, the commander of the 1st Chevauleger Regiment, Colonel Graf Wittgenstein, was mortally wounded.

164 Both regiments together only counted about 80 riders, who with the 50 remaining riders of the Saxon Chevauleger Regiments Prinz Clemens, formed the "Brigade etrangère" (Foreign Brigade) (Leyh, page 232).

165 Because of the significant shortage of horses, the Chevaulegers could hardly carry out a mounted attack and therefore had to fight on foot with their carbines.

6th Chevauleger Regiment especially distinguished itself by successfully defending against several attacks by Cossacks. The Bavarian regiments were not employed at the following Battle of Malo-Yaroslavetz; during the retreat after the fighting the Preysing Cavalry Division formed the rear guard of the 4th Army Corps on the march to Smolensk.

On 3 November a major battle ensued at Vyasma during the course of which the four Bavarian Chevaulegers regiments were employed on the point, the ends on both divisions of the 4th Army Corps. In the engagement, Preysing led an attack by the 5th and 6th Chevaulegers to relieve a hard-pressed Infantry division, and the 4th Chevauleger Regiment succeeded in repulsing a Russian dragoon regiment back into a swampy area where many Russian cavalrymen drowned. However, in these actions, the losses were so heavy that the four regiments were only able to form a squadron of 60 riders under Major von Zandt.

On 9 November 1812 on the march to Smolensk, the 4th Army Corps suffered considerable losses during the crossing of the Vop River from attacks by Platov's Cossacks. The Wiedenmann Light Battery had to leave its last cannons behind there. After this day, the Preysing division officially ceased to exist. The surviving officers und soldiers got in line individually or in small groups in the retreating flow. A few of these Chevaulegers were enlisted into the "*Escadron sacré*".[166]

From the organization of the Bavarian divisions at the beginning of the Russian campaign, one can conclude that the 13th Line Infantry Regiment and the 2nd Line Battery were detached and still deployed in the Danzig Fortress in 1811. Both Bavarian units were united there with three Polish and a Westphalian regiment to be the 7th Division (Grandjean) in Marshal MacDonald's 10th Army Corps. This corps formed the furthest left flank of the Grand Armeé and marched in the direction of the Duna River. In mid-July they formed a cordon there between Friedrichstadt and Daugavpils (Dünaburg). Until the retreat, the 13th Line Infantry Regiment did not have to fight once[167]; it was assembled at Friedrichstadt on 24 November and was pulled back to Bausk until 16 December 1812. On 18 December, the order was issued to withdraw to Tilsit, while on 26 December before the crossing of the Neman River the 13th Regiment did its first fighting against Russian units. After crossing the Neman at Ragnit, Marshal MacDonald learned of the Convention of Tauroggen, as consequence he lost his assigned Prussian division under York. MacDonald with the Bavarian troops made a forced march via Konigsberg and Elbing back to Danzig, which they reached on 17 January 1813.

So ended the campaign against Russia for the Bavarian forces. They went there with a total of 32,700 men including reinforcement, and about 30,000 remained there, i.e., never returned. About 60 percent of the officer corps never returned to Bavaria. Along with 5,800 horses, also 38 cannon, 260 munitions wagons, and about 300 other vehicles and 22 flags were lost.

The 1813 Campaign

The 13th Line Infantry Regiment, as opposed to the other Bavarian units did not suffer such heavy losses in the Russian campaign[168] and after the retreat from Russia together with two additional cannon of the 2nd Line Battery joined the garrison of the fortress at Danzig (Gdansk, Poland). Danzig, along with the city of Thorn (now Torun, Poland), would also play a role for the Bavarian units in 1813. Danzig was Napoleon's second defensive strong point on the Vistula. Under the command of Count Rapp, about 36,000 men from over 100 units could be assembled in Danzig.[169]

On 21 January, the encirclement of Danzig by Count Platov's forces began, and his forces were relieved the beginning of February by a detached Blockade Corps with about 10,000 men under Russian Lieutenant General Loevis. The Russian forces initially refrained from concerted attacks. The greatest losses by the Danzig garrison were therefore through sickness caused by poor hygienic conditions made more difficult by lack of provisions.[170] The Bavarian regiment was assigned to the main reserve of about 6,000 to 7,000 men that was composed of the garrison's remaining combat-capable units.

On 5 March, this main reserve force had to defend against a Russian surprise attack on the western outer defenses, and again on 24 March the Bavarians participated with Westphalian infantrymen in reinforcing the defensive works.

After these engagements, the Russian besiegers fell back into their inactivity that continued until June.[171] Due to the raging typhus epidemic the number of those suffering from the disease among the besieging forces rose to 10,000 dead by the end of May. Thanks to improvement of the climate in May, the units' numbers could be brought back up with convalescents, so the 13th Line

---

166 *This is according to Major General Preysing's diary (Leyh, page 240). For the composition of the "Escadron sacré" see the article in Napoleon Online (http://www.napoleon-online.de/html/1812_escadronsacre.html).*

167 *Colonel Graf Butler, who arrived from Polozk in mid-October as the new commander, was very favorably surprised at the appearance of the 13th Line Infantry Regiment: "I met the regiment in the best condition, the troops are healthy and rather well equipped with uniforms; what a difference from those regiments which I have just left and which hovered like ghosts in sickness!" (Quoted in Leyh, page 254).*

168 *On 17 January 1813, about 1,000 men arrived in Danzig (Leyh, page 283).*

169 *Among the units were, along with the Bavarian 13th Line Infantry Regiment, three Neapolitan regiments, three Polish regiments, a Westphalian regiment and numerous French replacement troops.*

170 *After only a short time, the city's hospital already had to care for about 15,000 men; the mortality rate rose continuously to finally reach 130 men per day (Leyh, page 286).*

171 *In the meantime, the Blockade Corps was strengthened to 30,000 men and Lieutenant General Loevis was relieved as commander by Duke Alexander of Wuerttemberg.*

The 4th Light Battalion in the fighting at Vilnius, 9 december 1812
Colored plate by A. Hoffmann, in the collection of M. Gärtner

Infantry Regiment again had 350 able-bodied men at the end of May.

On 9 June, the garrison attempted a major breakout on the west side with a total of 10,000 men and 50 cannon. Of the Bavarians, only the artillerymen were employed; the infantry remained located on the right wing in reserve. The breakout attempt failed, and on the same day the occupiers learned in the ceasefire between Napoleon and the Allies that had been concluded in the meantime on 4 June 1813. Based on the treaty the Russians were obligated to supply the garrison with adequate food provisions every five days.[172] On 24 August, the firing of twelve cannon announced the end of the ceasefire. At this time, the garrison strength was about 15,000 men, the Blockade Corps was reinforced to 40,000 men and the siege artillery increased to 202 cannon.[173]

After minor engagements in September[174] and the beginning of October, the Russian besiegers succeeded in taking control of heights from which they could bombard the city starting on 18 October. The bombardment lasted for several days at great intensity, which was followed by

---

172 These deliveries were supposed to be adequate for the strength of the garrison. However, Rapp demanded rations for 30,000 men at first, but the Duke of Wuerttemberg more realistically estimated the strength at 17,000 men and delivered the provisions, with short, conflict-driven interruptions, until the end of the ceasefire (Leyh, page 289).

173 During the ceasefire, excess officers, among them those returning Bavarian officers from the fortress, formed the "Roi du Rome" (King of Rome) elite regiment with 675 men, after the retreat from Russia.

174 Especially noteworthy here is the defense of a burning blockhouse by 40 infantrymen of the 13th Line Infantry Regiment under Captain Fahrbeck on 2 and 3 September. They had to defend against a numerically superior force that along with infantry fire also employed rockets and cannon against the blockhouse. After 17 hours without food or water and upper stories that had already caved in, Fahrbeck decided to break through to a 600-meter distant outer bastion. The breakout succeeded and the "heroes" were hailed by the entire garrison and as an honor the 15 Bavarian wounded were cared for in the palace by Count Rapp (Leyh, pages 290-292).

a renewed assault on the fortress by the Blockade Corps from the west on 1 and 2 November. After the end of November, Rapp saw himself forced to enter ceasefire negotiations. The beginning of November, the Bavarians had received the news that the kingdom had gone over to the Allies' side, whereupon the units initially were relieved of duty in the outposts and were stationed in the city. After numerous negotiations, the 13th Line Infantry Regiment with 383 infantrymen and 32 artillerymen could begin the march to their Bavarian homeland. They reached Bayreuth on 18 February.

Wrede's Bavarian Army Group returning from Russia along with arriving reinforcements was reorganized on the banks of the Vistula in January 1813.[175] As a result of the Convention of Tauroggen, the French and their allies had to leave East Prussia pull back in the direction of the Oder and Warthe rivers. The only Vistula fortresses remaining occupied were in Danzig and Thorn. In the latter city, the Bavarian 2nd Brigade under Major General Zoller entered the fortress under strong opposition by Wrede, in order to reinforce the garrison. The approximately 3,000 man division[176] was moved to the area of Posen (Poznan) and in the beginning of February its outposts had their first skirmishes with Russian units. On 7 February, General Wrede began the journey toward the Bavarian homeland and turned over command of the division to Major General Count (*Graf*) Rechberg.

The Russian advance forced France's and its allies' units to pull back to the Oder River. The Bavarian Division got the mission of covering this withdrawal. The Bavarians began their retreat on 11 February 1813 and reached the Oder at Krossen on 16 February. Because of further threats by Russian units that had captured Berlin in the meantime, the French felt compelled to retreat further to the Elbe River. On 27 February, the Bavarians began their withdrawal via Guben, Cottbus, Kalau and Grossenhain to Meissen, which the Division reached on 9 March with an effective strength of 113 officers, 1,700 men and 270 horses. The division guarded a long stretch of the Elbe's banks until they were ordered to Dresden on 23 March.[177] On 27 March, however, the Bavarians began another withdrawal to the west to the Mulde River which they reached at Rochlitz on 29 March. During this movement they had to defend themselves from an attack by three Russian squadrons. At the Mulde inside the village of Colditz the Russian cavalry attacked about 300 men of the three light infantry battalions. The Bavarians moved via Altenburg, Jena and Querfurt to Eisleben, where on 6 April 1813, von Rechberg received the orders from Lieutenant General von Raglovich to disband the division and have it return to Bavaria. The Bavarians traveled via Langensalza[178] and reached the Bavarian border at Coburg on 17 April and reached Bamberg with 1,040 man, 185 horsemen and one cannon on 18 April 1813.

The Bavarian Brigade[179], with its 4,150 men, which had received orders date 15 January 1813 to go to the Vistula fortress at Thorn, formed the bulk of the circa 4,700-man garrison. There were clashes with Russian units on a number of days in February, during which the siege ring around the fortress was closed. Like in Danzig, a large portion of the fortress' occupiers became sick with typhus[180] in February and March. At the beginning of April the besieging forces were strengthened to 17,000 men, so that on 10 April the bombardment could be conducted with four batteries. The Bavarian troops were able to repulse an attack by 200 Russian soldiers the following night. On 15 April, after additional bombardments of the fortress, there was another attack that brought the besiegers within 200 meters of the fortress walls and led to higher elevations in front of the city. Due to the given superiority in artillery fire, the commander decided on 15 April 1813 that it was necessary to capitulate. On 18 April, after giving up their weapons, the Bavarians marched out of the fortress and reached Hof on 16 June 1813 with 139 officers und 1,851 men.

On 10 March 1813, an order was issued to establish an Observation Corps with an authorized strength of 9,500 men[181] that would be put under the command of Lieutenant General von Raglovich. A decree of 14 March ordered the assignment of the infantry to two brigades commanded by Major General *Graf* (Count) Beckers and Colonel Maillot; the merging of the cavalry into a combined Chevauleger Regiment under Colonel von Seyffel and consolidation of the two batteries into an artillery division. However, this attempt at armament presented the training and logistics cadres with nearly unsolvable

---

175 *The contingent now consisted of a regiment with two infantry brigades (each with three light infantry battalions and three combined line infantry regiments with a battalion each), a cavalry regiment (three squadrons) and one artillery detachment (four batteries). As of 1 January 1813, both infantry brigades included a total of 231 officers and 3,608 men, the Combined Chevauleger Regiment had nine officers, 296 men and 294 horses (see Leyh, Anlage (Appendix) 13).*

176 *Consisting of the 1st Infantry Brigade with the 1st, 3rd and 6th Light Infantry Battalions, the 1st, 2nd and 3rd Combined Line Infantry Regiments, the Combined Chevauleger Regiment and a battery with six cannon.*

177 *In the meantime some officers and soldiers from the division were ordered to go home to strengthened Bavaria's national defense, so that the division only consisted of 13 companies (Leyh, page 274).*

178 *At that location, a detachment of the 2nd Silesian Hussar Regiment, having been notified by local inhabitants, attacked the Bavarian's Artillery and Transport Park and captured five cannon (Leyh, page 275).*

179 *Consisting of the 2nd, 4th and 5th Light Infantry Battalions and the 1st, 2nd and 3rd Combined Line Infantry Regiments of the brigade.*

180 *The number of sick personnel reached its high with 34 officers and 1,852 men on 18 March 1813 (Leyh, page 279).*

181 *The corps was supposed to be composed of ten infantry battalions with companies of 137 men, six squadrons of 125 horsemen and two batteries with 16 cannon (Leyh, page 297). However, it only reached an effective strength of about 8,000 men.*

problems.¹⁸² The Corps was hardly combat experienced due to the dominant number of newly raised soldiers, the few experienced men who were enlisted after the disbanding of Rechberg's division could not remedy these shortcomings.

At the end of March, the Observation Corp's forces were gathered in Franconia, with the 1st Brigade at Bayreuth, and the 2nd Brigade, cavalry and artillery at Bamberg. The exact organization of these forces at this time were:

Bavarian Observation Corps Lieutenant General von Raglovich		
1st Infantry Brigade Major General Graf Beckers	Combined Light Infantry Bn.	Parts of 3rd Light Infantry Bn.
		Parts of 4th Light Infantry Bn.
	1st Combined Line Infantry Regiment	II. Battalion 3rd Line Infantry
		Reserve 13th Line Infantry
	2nd Combined Line Infantry Regiment	II. Battalion 4th Line Infantry
		II. Battalion 8th Line Infantry
2nd Infantry Brigade Colonel Maillot de la Treille	Combined Light Infantry Bn.	Parts of 5th Light Infantry Bn
		Parts of 6th Light Infantry Bn
	1st Combined Line Infantry Regiment	II. Battalion 5th Line Infantry
		II. Battalion 7th Line Infantry
	2nd Combined Line Infantry Regiment	II. Battalion 9th Line Infantry
		II. Battalion 10th Line Infantry
Combined Chevauleger Regiment Colonel Graf Seyffel	1st Division	1st Squadron 1st Chevaulegers
		1st Squadron 2nd Chevaulegers
	2nd Division	1st Squadron 4th Chevaulegers
		1st Squadron 5th Chevaulegers
	3rd Division	1st. Squadron 3rd Chevaulegers
		1st Squadron 6th Chevaulegers
Artillery: Major Marabini 6-Pounder Foot Battery Weishaupt		6-Pounder Foot Battery Pamler

Based on the already strong anti-Napoleonic attitude in the Bavarian Army and officers corps, Raglovich attempted to mitigate the orders coming in from diverse French commanders and to keep his forces in or close to Bavaria as much as possible. Because of a personal letter from Napoleon to King Maximilian-Joseph on 20 April 1813, Raglovich had no other option but to comply with the French Commander-in-Chief's orders. His Observation Corps was to be designated as the "Royal Bavarian Division" ("*koeniglich bayerische Division*") effective 23 April and be assigned to Marshal Oudinot's 12th Corps.

On 29 April, the Raglovich Division crossed the Bavarian border and encamped at Graefental south of Saalfeld in Thuringia. The Bavarians proceeded by way of Jena and on 4 May reached Naumburg, where they received Napoleon's order to the 12th Corps to march in a southeasterly direction to Altenburg. From there the Bavarian Division went as the rear guard of the corps via Chemnitz, and Freiberg to Dresden, reaching its gates on 12 May 1813. After a parade by the 12th Army Corps in front of Napoleon on the following day, the Corps was deployed to Bischofswerda and thus came closer to employment at the Battle of Bautzen from 20 to 21 May.

Oudinot's 12th Corps was located in the outermost left flank of the French battle dispositions; the Bavarian Division¹⁸³ was assigned to the second line. As a result of the marked success of the first line, the Bavarians did not engage in the first day's fighting on 20 May. Also in the battle's second day, Oudinot kept the Bavarians in reserve, only the II. Battalion of the 3rd Line Infantry Regiment and the combined 3rd and 4th Light Infantry Battalion were assigned to the first line in the French divisions as support. The Bavarian artillery was assigned to the Corps' central artillery position and supported the movements of the infantry divisions with their fires. The Bavarian Division's losses after both days of this battle that was victorious for Napoleon came to 17 officers and 483 men.

The 12th Corps did not follow Napoleon's main army, but was to provide security for the left flank from Berlin. On 26 May, the Bavarians departed the encampment at Bautzen with the other divisions. On 28 May 1813, the Corps was attacked at Hoyerswerda by a combined Russian-Prussian unit under Major General von Borstell. During the engagement, four battalions of the 2nd Brigade were able to repulse an enemy attack. Only on 31 May did Oudinot set his Corps in motion to Torgau, but then on 2 June, he turned to the north toward Luckau. On 4 June, fighting occurred there but in which the Bavarian infantry was not engaged. In the evening, a detachment of 6 Prussian and 2 Russian squadrons bypassed an infantry division and ran into Bavarian Chevaulegers who were deployed to protect another division. Two squadrons, together with two additional squadrons of

---

182 *From a report by General Raglovich, one can infer that "the artillery was in the best condition, only the supply of ammunition and transport means seemed too limited. The cavalry appeared like the infantry to have excellent morale; but they could neither ride nor wield a saber, not to mention that the horses could not stand the firing [of weapons], so the cavalry could not be used at all for skirmishing. The infantry battalions were thoroughly incomplete; officers were especially lacking; in one battalion for example there were only four officers; the NCOs were generally of no use; there were Feldwebels who had only served 10 months. The troops had not been trained, ... one had still not even fired at a target. The sharpshooters did not know the signals and had no idea how to skirmish" (from Gerneth/Kiessling, 2. Teil, page 466).*

183 *At this time the division counted 5,350 infantrymen, 630 cavalrymen and 16 cannon (Leyh, page 304).*

Hesse-Darmstadt cavalry were overrun and fled. The commander of the Bavarian Chevaulegers, Colonel Seyffel, then had the two remaining squadrons attack – in closed formation - the flank of the enemy cavalry and push them back in turn.

When the ceasefire went into effect on 4 June 1813, the Bavarian Division in conjunction with the 12th Corps, went into quarters around Herzberg. On 20 June and 10 July, both individual supply trains arrived at the division there with clothing and equipment from Bavaria.

When the ceasefire expired, the Bavarians along with an approximately 70,000-man army group under Marshal Oudinot were to march in the direction of Berlin. On 15 August, Oudinot gathered these forces at Baruth and on 19 August began the advance.[184] On the evening of 20 August, the Bavarian Division was attacked by about 2,000 Cossacks at Luckenwalde, who were driven off by the fires of a light infantry battalion and the Bavarian artillery. At the Battle of Grossbeeren on 25 August 1813, the 12th Corps arrived too late to get decisively engaged and could only stop the enemy cavalry that was pursuing the fleeing French. During the ensuing retreat to the Wittenberg fortress, the Bavarians got the task of escorting the Army Group's large artillery park. On 3 September, the Army Group reached Wittenberg, where on 4 September, Marshal Ney took over command of the group, which consisted of three Corps with another circa 65,000 men. On 5 September after the group began its eastward advance toward Jueterbog, the Bavarians in the 12th Corps ran into units of the Prussian Tauentzien *Landwehrkorps* (Militia Corps), which withdrew to Jueterbog after a fight.

On the following day, Ney pursued the retreating Prussian units with his army group and the movement developed into the Battle of Dennewitz. The Bavarians were detached from the 12th Corps and ordered to provide cover for the large artillery park behind the battle line. When the French order started to waver from Prussian General Buelow's maneuvering, a Bavarian battery had to support it with defensive fires and itself received the 9th Line Infantry's II Battalion for protection. In the face of concerted attacks, the battalion formed a square and took some of the cannon along with artillerymen into its center. However, a Prussian hussar regiment succeeded in penetrating the square so that most of the Bavarian infantrymen and artillerymen and their cannon were captured.

The remainder of the artillery park assigned to the Bavarian Division wound up in the maelstrom of the general flight/stampede. Indeed Raglovich had his units form battalion squares and created a large division square on all sides of the artillery park. In this formation the Bavarians succeeded in an orderly withdrawal in a southeasterly direction. On 8 September they crossed the Elbe at Torgau and then the Bavarians gathered with the remainder of the 12th Corps at Eilenburg halfway from Torgau to Leipzig.[185]

20 September, after the 12th Corps was disbanded, the Bavarian Division left Torgau where it had returned and marched upstream along the Elbe reaching Dresden on 23 September 1813. Starting on 6 October, the Bavarian Division, commanded by General Maillot, followed Napoleon's main army down the Elbe and served as the security force for the imperial headquarters during the advance. The division moved via Meissen, Oschatz and Wurzen to Dueben west of Torgau, but then got orders from Napoleon to march to the southwest to Leipzig.

The Bavarian Division remained 25 kilometer northeast of Leipzig in Eilenburg, to enable the main army's large artillery park to cross the Mulde. The Bavarians also remained at this location during the Battle of Nations at Leipzig and took over guarding a large artillery and wagon park. On 20 October 1813, after the battle, Maillot with his Bavarian troops led the wagon park to Torgau and had his troops camp outside the fortress awaiting further orders. On 22 October, after Maillot received a personal letter from Tsar Alexander, which confirmed that Bavaria had joined the Allies' side, the division marched to Leipzig and reached Bamberg, on Bavarian soil, on 8 November.

---

184 *During the consolidation phase on 17 August, the Bavarian Chevaulegers on picket duty were surprised by a detachment of Prussian hussars and lost not just 86 horses but also their commander, Colonel Seyffel, who was captured by the Prussians (Leyh, page 313).*

185 *The days from 5 to 8 September cost the Raglovich Division approximately 2,000 casualties. After sending several hundred officers and soldiers back to Bavaria, the division numbered about 2,300 men who were assigned to four battalions, one squadron with 141 horses and one battery (Leyh, page 318).*

SOURCES AND LITERATURE

Bayerisches Kriegsarchiv, D**er Bayerische Soldat im Felde,** 1st volume, Munich 1898.

Behringer, L., **Die Uniformen der Bayerischen Armee 1682 bis 1848**, München, 1848.

Bezzel, Dr. Oskar, **Geschichte des Königlich-Bayerisches Heeres unter König Max I. Joseph von 1806 bis 1815**, Munich, Max Schick, 1933.

Brauer, Hans, **Bayerische Infanterie 1803-1815**, Part 1, Brauer Bogen Nr. 13

Brauer, Hans, **Bayerische Kavallerie**, Brauer Bogen Nr. 90

Brauer, Hans, **Bayerische Fahnen 1777-1815**, Part 1 and 2, Brauer Bogen Nr. 18

Brauer, Hans, **Formation, Ausrüstung und Taktik der Bayerischen Infanterie 1804/14**, Appeared in the information in the hand-colored Knötel-Brauer "Uniformbogen", Enclosure to **Zeitschrift für Heereskunde**, Nr. 43-45, 1932.

Bunde, Peter, **BRIGADE-Uniformtafeln**, (Brigade Uniform Plates), self-published, www.brigade-uniform-tafeln.de

Cantler, J.B., **Der bayerischen Armee sämtliche Uniformen von 1800-1873**, Published on Napoleon Online (http,//www.napoleon-online.de/html/cantler. html).

Charrie, Pierre, **Drapeaux et Etendards**, Paris, Leopard d'Or, 1982.

Dauer, Josef, **Das königlich Bayerische 10. Infanterie-Regiment Prinz Ludwig**, Volume 4, 1778-1813, Ingolstadt, A. Ganghofer, 1901.

Döderlein, von, **Geschichte des königlich Bayerischen 8. Infanterie-Regiments (Prankh)**, Part 2, 1805-1825, Landshut, 1893.

Fabrice, F. von, **Das königlich Bayerische 6. Infanterie-Regiments Kaiser Wilhelm, König von Preußen**, Part 2, 1805 bis 1835, Munich, Verlag J. F. Nietsch, 1896.

Fuhrmann, Rolf, **Bayerische Linieninfanterie im Feldzug 1809**, Appeared in **Figuren International** No 29 and in Furtenbach, Friedrich von, Die Generale des Bayerischen Heeres im Feldzuge gegen Rußland 1812/13, Appeared in the illustrations in the **Bayerischen Kriegs- und Heeresgeschichte**, Vol. 21, Munich, Lindauer, 1912.

Gerneth and Kießling, **Geschichte des königliche Bayerischen 5. Infanterie-Regiments (vacant Großherzog Ludwig IV. von Hessen)**, 2 Volumes, Berlin, 1883-1893.

Geschichte des k.B. I. Infanterie-Regiments König seit seiner Errichtung im Jahre 1778 nebst einer Vorgeschichte seiner Stammregimenter, Without location or year.

Hammer, Benedikt, **Waffen der bayerischen Armee 1800 bis 1830**, from http,//www.bayerischewaffen.de/wa-1800.htm.

Heilmann, F., **Der Bayerische Soldat im Felde**, Munich, 1853.

Heinze, E., **Geschichte des kgl. Bayer. 6. Chevaulegers-Regiments „Prinz Albrecht von Preußen" 1803 bis 1871 sowie der Stammabteilungen des Regiments**, Leipzig 1898.

Hemmann, Thomas / Stein, Markus, **Le troisième régiment de chevau-légers royal bavarois « Leiningen » lors de la campagne de 1809**, Appeared in **Soldats Napoléoniens**, No. 23, 2009.

Hess, Peter von, „**Schlachtengalerie**", Residenz

Käuffer, **Geschichte des königlich bayerischen 9. Infanterie-Regiments Wrede**, Würzburg, Verlag Ballhorn und Cramer, 1895.

Knötel, Richard, **Große Uniformkunde**, 1053 plates, Rathenow, M. Babenzien, 1890–1914.

Knötel, Richard, **Mittheilungen der militärischen Tracht**, Berlin, 1895-1910.

Königlich-Baierisches Regierungsblatt, Munich 1812, Unterricht in den Waffen-Uebungen für die Infanterie der königlich-baierischen National-Garde III. Klasse im Isar-Kreise, Munich, 1814.

Kraus, Jürgen, **Die bayerische Armee 1822**, Ingolstadt, Deutsche Gesellschaft für Heereskunde, 2011

Leyh, Max, **Die Feldzüge des Königliche Bayerischen Heeres unter Max I. Joseph von 1805 bis 1815**, Sechster Band, 2, Teil der Geschichte des Bayerischen Heeres, Munich, Max Schick, 1935.

Lienhart, Constant and Humbert, René, **Les Uniformes de l'armee francaise depuis 1690 jusqu'a nos jours**, Leipzig, Ruhl, 1895-1906.

Müller, Karl / Braun, Louis, **Die Organisation, Bekleidung, Ausrüstung der kgl. Bayer. Armee 1806-1906**, Munich, A. Oehrleins Verlag, 1899.

Münich, Friedrich, **Geschichte der Entwicklung der bayerischen Armee seit zwei Jahrhunderten**, Munich, J. Lindauer'sche Buchhandling (Schöpping), 1864.

Perrot, Aristide M., **Historische Sammlung aller noch bestehenden Ritterorden der verschiedenen Nationen, nebst einer chronologischen Uebersicht der erloschenen Ritterorden**, Leipzig 1821, Nachdruck, Dortmund, Baumgärtner Verlag, 1980.

Pivka, Otto von (Smith, Digby), **Napoleons German Allies (4) - Bavaria**, London, Osprey Men-at-Arms No. 106, 1979.

Rangliste der königlich-baierschen Armee für das Jahr 1811, Munich, 1811.

Ruith, Max / Ball, Emil, **Kurze Geschichte des k. B. Infanterie-Regiments Prinz Karl von Bayern**, Augsburg, Selbstverlag, 1890.

Sauzey, Colonel Camille, **Les Allemands sous les Aigles Francaises. Nos Allies les Bavarois**, Volume 5., Paris, Editions Art et Science, 1953.

Schubert, **Königlich Bayerisches 13. Infanterie-Regiment Kaiser Franz Josef von Österreich**, Ingolstadt, 1906.

Stein, Markus / Bunde, Peter, **L'Infanterie bavaroise pendant la campagne de Russie 1812**, Appeared in Soldats Napoléoniens, No. 1, 2004 (German Translation on Napoleon Online, http,//www.napoleon-online.de/armee_bayern_infanterie1812.html).

Ulrich, Maximilian, **Die Königs-Chevaulegers**, Gedenkblätter aus der Geschichte des kgl. Bayerischen 4. Chevaulegers-Regimentes „König", No location, Bondi (publisher), 1892.

Weiß, Hans-Karl, **Die Bayerische Bewaffnung mit dem kleinen Gewehr 1800-1815**, Published on Napoleon Online (http,//www.napoleon-online.de/html/bay_infwaffen.html).

Xylander, Rudolf Ritter von, **Geschichte des 1. Feldartillerie-Regiments Prinz-Regent Luitpold**, 2 Volumes, Berlin, E.S. Mittler, 1905-1909.

Markus Gärtner
Markus Stein
Peter Bunde (Illustration)

Translated by Richard L. Sanders

The Saxon Army 1810-1813

No army of the German Confederation of the Rhine underwent such fundamental changes in organization and uniforms as did the Saxon forces of the Napoleonic era. Based on the experiences from the 1806-07 campaigns on Prussia's side and 1809 allied with the French, the Saxon Army undertook extensive reforms.

This book presents this "new" Saxon Army with numerous contemporary illustrations, with plates by Patrice Courcelle and Edmund Wagner as well as graphic tables of uniforms of all the regiments by Peter Bunde. A description of the war experiences rounds out the presentation and thus the volume gives the reader a good, thorough introduction to the organization, uniforms and history of the Saxon Army of 1810-1813.

72 pages; Paperback, 51 color illustrations, including three maps and 15 full-page plates with uniformsn and flags.

English edition of "*Die Sächsische Armee 1810-1813*".

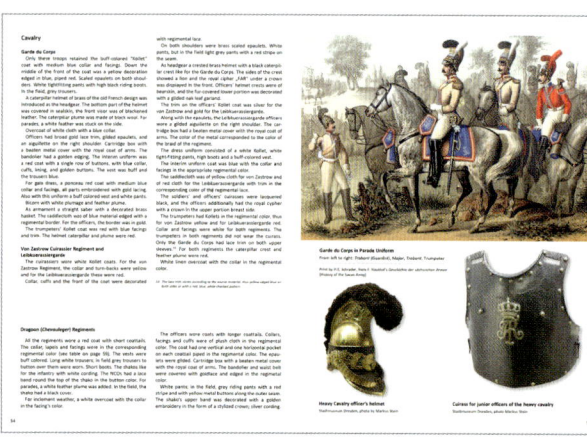